UFO

On a November morning in 1953 Flying Officer G. Smythe and Flying Officer T. S. Johnson, patrolling at 2,000 feet in a Vampire jet from West Malling, spotted a brilliant object stationary in the sky at their own height.

Suddenly shooting into motion, it passed above them at terrific speed.

When they reported their findings to Fighter Command HQ, it became the subject of a facetious exchange in the House of Commons. The then Parliamentary Secretary to the Defence Ministry offered no explanation other than that meteorological balloons were up at that time.

One MP quipped that it was "all ballooney".

Was it?

Then why should two trained professional airmen have boobed over a balloon?

And why were the findings of their two-hour interrogation logged "confidential" and the details never disclosed?

Unidentified Flying Objects

Robert Chapman

A Mayflower Paperback

UNIDENTIFIED FLYING OBJECTS
Robert Chapman

First published by Arthur Barker Ltd 1969

Published as a Mayflower Paperback 1970

Mayflower Paperbacks are published by
Mayflower Books,
3 Upper James Street, London, W.1.
Made and printed in Great Britain by
Hunt Barnard & Co. Ltd., Aylesbury, Bucks.

Contents

Appreciation

I should like to record my grateful thanks to my friends Charles Bowen and Gordon Creighton for helping me prepare material for this book and especially for permission to quote from *Flying Saucer Review*.

Foreword

You are sitting in the garden watching the sun go down. Daylight is fading and all you can hear is the twitter of birds. In the warmth of the summer evening you feel quite drowsy. Then suddenly you are wide awake. But can you believe your eyes?

From nowhere, streaking across the sky, comes a shadowy silver disc with an orange glow round the rim.

It makes no noise. For a moment it hovers high in the sky. Then, without warning, it swoops away and disappears into the distance at an incredible speed. Suddenly you have joined the growing crowd of people who can claim to have seen a flying saucer.

It is more than twenty years since flying saucers got off to a flying start near Mount Rainier, Washington, although they had been seen in different guises at different places long before. And still they come.

Since June 1947, the birthday of the Unidentified Flying Object, to use its modern and more dignified title, many thousands of sighting reports have been collected by enthusiastic saucerers in London and elsewhere. UFOs have been spotted from Axminster to Adelaide, Brighton to Bangkok, Manchester to Memphis.

It is probable indeed that not a day goes by without a saucer report being broadcast or published in some newspaper somewhere on earth. Many are not particularly inspiring; they are forgotten next day. But at other times (quite regularly in fact) we have a real saucer 'flap' which excites a whole country and starts telephone bells trilling round the world, which draws crowds to the scene, calls out the police and mobilizes nearby Service units. It is with some of the 'flaps' which have stirred and stimulated the stolid people of Britain that this book is mainly concerned.

It is freely admitted that many saucer sightings are quickly explained away (some perhaps too quickly) as hoaxes or commonplace aircraft observed under curious conditions or from odd angles. But there is thought to be a large and growing total of sightings which stubbornly refuse to be explained away; and there is certainly a growing suspicion among intelligent men and women, including doctors, lawyers, journalists, businessmen and scientists that Government officials know more about the phenomena than they are prepared to admit: that information is deliberately being withheld in the mistaken belief that this is in the public interest.

Some of the people who have seen UFOs for themselves are expert observers – policemen, coastguards, air-line pilots and weather forecasters – whose testimony one is obliged to take seriously. They are certainly not cranks and would hardly be likely to indulge in leg-pulling.

What, from their evidence, seems undeniable is that from time to time objects appear in the sky and even on or near the ground which cannot be explained in simple terrestrial terms. Nor, from this, can one escape the notion that a percentage of UFOs *may* come from outer space under the direction of intelligent beings from other worlds.

The likelihood or otherwise of this being so must be left for later discussion. In the meantime, however, and since humanity as a whole is becoming increasingly space conscious, it is as well to bear in mind the relationship of our world with the universe at large.

We live on a beautiful but otherwise rather insignificant planet dependent for its livelihood on a pretty unimportant star (the sun) on the edge of a vast island or galaxy of stars called the Milky Way. In this galaxy are millions of stars with even more millions of planets going round them in much the same way as our earth goes round the sun. And out beyond the Milky Way, extending further than the most powerful earthbound telescope can peer, are millions more galaxies comprising billions more solar systems.

The notion therefore that the planet Earth is unique does not make sense at all. The much more likely probability is that there are many thousands of earths so similar to the one we know that some form of intelligent life must have evolved on them. Of course there are snags in this reasoning, but it will do for the time being. The point to be made here is that it is against this infinitely vast and bewildering cosmic background of which we know so little that the mystery of UFOs has to be considered. Against this, surely *nothing* is impossible!

One thing more: the human race, in an incredibly short period of time, has found the means of leaving earth and going to the moon. If a lunar landing is not achieved either by the Russians or Americans this year (1969) it will certainly be achieved next year, or the year after. And then the planets, Mars, Venus, Jupiter will be visited. So if at any time in our history we have been considered 'interesting' by some unimaginably superior intelligence out there in the universe, surely it must be since the second world war, and more particularly now.

I

The Flying Cross

It was 4 a.m. on a chilly morning in October 1967. Mr Christopher Garner of Marshwood Farm, Hatherleigh near Exeter, Devon, was fast asleep, tucked up in a blanket in his Land-Rover just off a main road on the edge of Dartmoor. After a long drive he had stopped for a few hours before continuing his journey home.

Suddenly he was aroused by someone knocking on the side window. Mr Garner awoke dazed and was startled to find a flashlight flooding into his driving cabin. When he had collected his wits he saw the face of a policeman staring in through the glass. Wondering what the devil was up Mr Garner opened the door prepared to protest his innocence of whatever the Law accused him. The thought may have occurred to him that a Dartmoor prisoner had escaped and the police were checking the area, but the constable's manner soon put him in an easier state of mind.

The man was plainly not prepared for trouble nor intent on making any. After apologizing, he asked if Mr Garner would mind doing him a favour.

'What's that?'

The motorist eased himself out of the Land-Rover into the frosty roadway and saw that a police car had pulled up behind his own vehicle with another police officer standing beside it. The first policeman pointed away to the dark horizon. There was something out there, he said, that he would like Mr Garner to take a look at and thus witness that the two constables were not 'seeing things'.

Following the man's outstretched arm, Mr Garner saw what appeared to be a collection of pulsating lights in the sky and, as he looked, the lights formed into a cross and began to move off into the distance.

This was the beginning of a saucer 'flap' which lasted the

best part of a week. In a few hours the whole country knew about it. Morning paper headlines proclaimed:

'Z CAR CHASES STAR SPANGLED UFO FOR 14 MILES' ... 'POLICE CHASE FLYING CROSS' ... 'THE FLYING THING LEAVES TWO CONSTABLES BAFFLED' etc.

It appeared that the two patrolmen – Constables Clifford Waycott and Roger Willey – had been driving along the A3072 between Okehampton and Holsworthy when they saw the 'Thing' in the sky behaving almost as if it had spotted *them* and was watching to see what they would do. It was a little way ahead to their left. It was not so bright that it hurt the eyes but it had a distinct glow, and the way it sailed silently along the dark treetops ruled out any notion that it was any kind of conventional aircraft.

The policemen radioed their headquarters that they had spotted some kind of unidentified flying object and were going to investigate. As they moved forward the 'Thing' also seemed to move as though deliberately keeping its distance; the faster they travelled the faster it sped ahead until at times they found themselves doing nearly ninety miles an hour. The squad car flashed round corners, streaked up hills and swooped down valleys trying to keep up but the nearest Waycott and Willey got to it was four hundred yards.

When it appeared they were never going to catch up, the driver sensibly slackened speed and gave up the chase. Neither of them fancied having to report that they had crashed a police car in pursuit of a flying saucer!

The whole incident got splendid Press coverage, refuting the oft-repeated complaint that newspapers were no longer interested in UFOs or were inclined to ridicule sightings while submitting to a mysterious form of government censorship. This sighting was different. It was really worth going to town over.

At a Press conference later in the day PC Waycott said: 'The light wasn't piercing but it was very bright. It was star-spangled – just like looking through wet glass – and although we reached ninety miles an hour it accelerated away from us'.

Before the 'Thing' disappeared, the constables said, it was joined by a second object which was also large, cross-shaped, extremely bright and noiseless. Both men spoke of the remarkable speed of the objects – especially the first one. 'It seemed to know we were chasing it,' they reported.

The RAF station at nearby Chivenor quickly denied that the Flying Cross could have anything to do with them. They knew of no aircraft that could fit the description given by the constables let alone match its performance, flying slower than fifty miles an hour, hovering and then making off at supersonic speed. Nor could anyone else at the time offer a suggestion to explain the object. Not, that is, in familiar terms.

During the next few days more and more people reported seeing flying crosses along with other aerial objects shaped like cigars and catherine wheels. A whole circus of fantastic flying machines seemed to be taking to the night sky over Britain. Within the first forty-eight hours more than a dozen reliable witnesses had spoken up, including more policemen and some BBC engineers manning a transmitter on Dartmoor.

A 'fiery cross' was seen by half a dozen police officers over Glossop, Derbyshire. A Brighton bus driver saw a cigar-shaped object over the coast at Saltdean, Sussex, which, he said, had a bright green glow and sparks coming from the tail. A Scottish coastguard claimed to have observed a 'silver cartwheel' over Wigtownshire. 'It came from the west and was travelling at about four hundred miles an hour,' he reported. 'There was a faint dynamo hum coming from it. I watched it for about ten minutes until it disappeared over the horizon in the north-east.'

Then there was retired RAF Wing Commander Eric Cox driving with his wife from Cadham to Fordingbridge, Hampshire. Both were startled to see seven bright lights in formation in the night sky. At first the lights formed a perfect V but later rearranged themselves into a cross. 'They certainly seemed to be under some sort of control – the formation was perfect,' said the Wing Commander. 'The night was clear with the moon just coming up and we were stone cold sober.'

The flying lights made no noise, he said. All seven were about the same size and whitish-yellow in appearance. It was impossible to estimate their speed as they flew away over the treetops. 'You just cannot believe these things until you see them,' the Wing Commander said. Exactly what the lights were he could not guess, but it was not long before an explanation was forthcoming – an explanation that saucer researchers are always dismally prepared for.

It seemed that all the objects seen in the sky during October 25, 26 and 27, the night of the flap, could be attributed to the planet Venus which astronomers at the Royal Observatory, Herstmonceux, Sussex said was extremely bright in the eastern sky in the early morning at this time of year. The explanation was clearly good enough for Mr George Terry, Chief Constable of East Sussex, who, after hearing reports from nine of his officers, summed up his conclusions thus:

'I am satisfied that what was seen was either Venus or an artificial satellite reflecting light from the moon.'

The Venus-satellite explanation, however, did not last long. It was almost immediately challenged by Mr Peter Baker, an amateur astronomer of Hastings who, it appeared, had been asked by the Observatory to look into the Flying Cross sightings. Mr Baker put the kybosh on Venus by reporting that he had spotted a UFO *below cloud level* and in a position which ruled out any connection with the planet.

This drew from the Observatory the dramatic statement that: 'There is something up there which is not a star or a planet.'

The information was promptly passed to the Meteorological Office and the Ministry of Defence, and the mystery deepened. The Ministry denied emphatically that the UFO sightings could be accounted for by any new aircraft under test. But they could not offer any alternative explanation. Somebody else could however – the Rev Lawrence Inge of Stourton Caundle, near Sherborne.

Mr Inge, who had seen a formation of lights in the sky at seven p.m., came up with an explanation that seemed more than adequate to explain away the Flying Cross if not the other October sightings.

'There was one very bright light surrounded by seven or eight white lights, some of which were flashing,' he said. 'The lights were travelling in the form of a cross and at the same speed. It immediately came to me that these were planes flying in close formation, but I was puzzled by the one very bright light in the middle. Then, suddenly, it dawned on me. It was a tanker plane with other aircraft round it taking part in refuelling exercises.'

This explanation was heartily endorsed by the Ministry of Defence who said that there had been mid-air refuelling exercises by the US Air Force over the West Country. Not only that. It also appeared that the Americans had been carrying out similar exercises over Scotland. Nobody had remembered this at the time, but now it was recalled that four bombers and a tanker had made mid-air connections by night on at least three occasions over southern England alone.

A United States spokesman added the detail that their refuelling exercises had been carried out at an altitude of 26,000 feet and explained: 'A lot of light is needed during these operations and the tanker has a string of lights along the fuselage shining under its belly all the time.'

So it seemed we could all relax – provided we were prepared to forget the cigar-shaped objects and 'catherine wheels' and to overlook the fact that a Flying Cross had been seen by policemen at Glossop where no refuelling exercises had taken place. But readers of the *Sunday Express* may remember a front page headline at the end of the week which stated:

'UFO RIDDLE – BACK TO SQUARE ONE'

'The Great UFO mystery is again wide open,' the newspaper said. 'The Ministry of Defence admitted yesterday that the emphatic and official explanation given on Friday – that the objects seen in the sky were US Air Force planes refuelling in mid-air – no longer stands up.

'There were no refuelling operations at the time of the sightings. A USAF spokesman said all these exercises were between five p.m. and nine p.m. And all the sightings of "fiery crosses" in the sky (most by patrolling policemen) were between midnight and dawn.'

Confronted by that evidence, the Ministry of Defence had said: 'The refuelling theory obviously can't account for the early morning sightings now. It looks as though there is still no rational explanation for the objects the policemen report having seen.'

And as if to confound the issue still further, the Flying Cross turned up again and was watched for several minutes by former police officer Mr Frederick Smith of Grinstead Lane, Lancing, Sussex. Mr Smith and his wife both saw it at five-thirty a.m. It was in the shape of the cross of Lorraine, they said, a really wonderful sight. And while the Smiths were observing it a policeman at Bacup, Lancs, saw a cigar-shaped object hovering high over the police station. Constable Brian Earnshaw had heard a crackling over the station's short-wave radio and gone outside to examine the aerial. Looking up, he had seen a UFO hovering, he said, two hundred and fifty feet above the station roof.

'It was approximately fifty feet long,' he reported, 'and ten feet in diameter. There were portholes along the side but no visible signs of propulsion. The ship appeared to be metallic and gave off a bright glow. There was a low whirring sound coming from it.'

Two other policemen, Colin Donahoe and Malcolm Reader, also claimed to have seen the UFO which, they said, remained in full view for several minutes before rising vertically and disappearing. Later a statement was issued by the Lancashire police, which read: 'We have had UFO reports before – but nothing like this. There has been no reasonable explanation but it was something definitely seen.'

Nor was that the end. The October flap was dying hard. On Monday October 30, the *Daily Express*, under the headline, 'LOOK, IT'S A UFO', reported:

> 'Four policemen and a clergyman saw UFOs over the weekend. So did a housewife and two farmers. And many others.
>
> 'From all over the country reports flooded in: "Great balls of fire" . . . "A flying cross of Lorraine" . . . "Cigar-shaped" . . .
>
> 'Methodist minister, the Rev Ian Haile of Truro, Cornwall saw a "flying cross". He watched it for three minutes.
>
> 'Police constable Michael Sands and two colleagues were changing shifts at five-twenty a.m. at Lancing, West Sussex, when they spotted an object.
>
> ' "It looked like a silver pinpoint of light," said PC Sands, "moving rapidly across the sky."
>
> 'Farmers John Brown and Mervyn Hurst were tending cattle at Boscastle, Cornwall, when "a ball of fire appeared in the sky."
>
> 'On Dartmoor, at Princetown, four schoolboys saw TWO objects – "a flying cross and a cigar-shaped light".
>
> 'Southampton policeman John Whitcombe saw a UFO while driving through Portsmouth with his family. "Like a

rugby ball or a fat saucer, so bright I had to shield my eyes." And Mrs Jeffrey Clayton, wife of a bank clerk in Stoke Newington saw two white fingers of light, vertical in the sky. "Then they turned, closed together and shot like a rocket to the East . . ." '

The flap that began with the first sighting of the Flying Cross by the two Devon policemen marked the peak point in the biggest total of UFO sighting reports in the British Isles for ten years. Altogether in 1967 the Ministry of Defence checked on 362 reports from people in all walks of life and from all parts of the country. This total was three times higher than usual. The next highest total, for example, was a mere ninety-five in the previous year and back in 1959 there were only twenty-two.

The October flap led by Mr Peter Mills, Conservative MP for Torrington, Devon, to ask two pertinent questions in the Commons. The first requested the Secretary of State for Defence to 'make a statement on the circumstances in which an unidentified flying object has been seen in the Okehampton area of Devon and say what are his plans to deal with a recurrence of this flying object.' Mr Mills also asked whether the flying object, described as a star-shaped cross larger than a conventional aircraft, was a British aircraft or an unidentified flying object.

In reply Mr Merlyn Rees, Under Secretary of State for Defence for the Royal Air Force, said: 'We received a number of reports of objects seen in the sky over North Devon in October. After investigation some proved to be aircraft and some were lights. Of the lights, the majority were the planet Venus but the source of a few lights has not been positively identified.'

He added: 'I can say, however, that none of these unidentified lights was an alien object. There are standing instructions for RAF stations to report unusual objects seen in the sky and standing arrangements for investigating these reports and similar reports from other sources. I do not consider additional action necessary.'

Mr Mills, who clearly found the reply less than satisfactory, then asked: 'Will the Hon Gentleman bear in mind that this matter is not only of considerable interest to the South-West, but also of some concern? How does this statement square with the statements of two police officers and of engineers at Hessary Tor that low flying objects were moving for over an hour in the area?'

Mr Rees: '. . . I have published details of all the investigations which have been made over recent years, and none of these would give any reason to believe that there are unidentified objects in the sense that has been implied. Further, we have complete radar coverage to a very great height over all these islands and have access to that over Europe, and none of this leads us to believe in any sense that there is anything else that we know nothing about.'

Mr Rees was then asked if he could give assurance that the Ministry of Defence received scientific advice about UFO sightings?

'I can give that assurance,' he said. 'This is not just an air defence matter. We have access to scientists of high repute – they have been consulted on all these matters – and also to psychologists.'

On the subject of radar coverage Mr Rees was asked if he could explain the contents of a letter from his department in which it was stated that a certain object 'might or might not' have been an aircraft.

His reply was that inquiries about UFOs often came weeks after the sighting when the trail was cold and investigation difficult. But nothing, he added, led the Ministry of Defence to think that any unexplained objects were space ships piloted by 'men from Mars or anything of that kind.'

As might be expected the mention of Mars provoked laughter and Mr Shinwell seized the opportunity to say: 'Would it not be desirable for the Government to encourage this idea that there are unidentified flying objects and a danger of invasion from another planet? Would this not create the necessary diversion so that people in this country, and the electors in particular, would not worry about their economic problems?'

Mr Rees: 'Judging from the public's response to some newspaper reports, I can only hope that they will take my Right Hon Friend's remark seriously!'

In these few sentences the whole subject of UFOs, whether seen over Britain or elsewhere, was virtually dismissed as nonsense. But if MPs, or the majority of them, were satisfied, there were a good many other people who were not. What *was* the Flying Cross? Had it after all been listed as an ordinary aircraft or group of aircraft refuelling? If so, how was one to account for the fact that the aircraft made no noise? How was one to account for the fact that they were seen hovering just above the treetops? And what about the astonishing burst of speed that took them out of sight, to say nothing of the *second* cross which Constables Willey and Waycott reported seeing.

Surely the Flying Cross could not be ascribed to some new and curious manifestation of the planet Venus, however brightly it may have shone? Venus does not normally skim over treetops and police officers accustomed to patrolling at night, especially in open country, must have seen the planet many times before – far too often, one would have thought, to have been misled into chasing it!

To my mind, whatever explanations may be found for other sightings during the October flap, the only category to which the Flying Cross can be reasonably ascribed is that of the few lights which Mr Rees said had 'not been positively identified'. That, as the *Sunday Express* said, puts the UFO mystery back to square one. Readers may remember that when Constables Willey and Waycott were interviewed in a television programme more than six months after the October flap, they were still very puzzled by what they had seen. Both said they would willingly accept any explanation that seemed at all plausible but in fact nothing had been put forward to account for the sighting satisfactorily.

Whether the Flying Cross will ever be explained in familiar terms it is not possible to predict. But one thing one can feel sure about is that, whatever it was, it was *seen*, and by competent observers. It was not simply imagined. Had it been seen by day instead of in darkness there might have been no mystery at all although it is difficult to think of any ordinary flying object which would normally behave in the way described by the policemen.

This particular point is made here in view of an even more extraordinary report of a sighting in broad daylight not so very far from where the Flying Cross first appeared. It did not get as much publicity at the time, but it had many features in common with the Okehampton sighting.

2

The Moigne Downs 'Craft'

The report came from Mr J. B. W. (Angus) Brooks, a former Comet Flight Administration Officer with BOAC. Mr Brooks, a family man in his fifties, is a prime example of a man of common sense who would not dream of inventing a sighting for the sake of personal publicity and has no history of suffering from hallucinations.

The report he submitted was not prepared without thought and contained the kind of details one would expect from a man skilled in administrative problems and familiar with intelligence work. He was, in fact, engaged on intelligence work with the Royal Air Force during the war. It went like this:

REPORT OF UFO OBSERVED AT MOIGNE DOWNS 1½ MILES NORTH OF RINGSTEAD BAY BETWEEN WEYMOUTH AND LULWORTH COVE, DORSET, ENGLAND BY ANGUS BROOKS.

Date of Observation: 26.10.67. Time: 11.25 a.m. to 11.47 a.m. British Summer Time.
Position: Grid Ref 755833 ordnance survey map (1 inch/1 mile) Gt Britain Sheet 178 (Dorchester).
Weather at Time: Clear sky with small amount of low cloud. Wind: SSW Force 8 (+—)

The report was of a UFO unlike any other described up to that time which Mr Brooks claimed to have seen while out walking with his dogs and which he sketched immediately after the sighting. Mr Brooks' story was that he saw the UFO while lying on his back to shelter from a high wind in a shallow trough on the hillside. He had hardly had time to position himself with his hands behind his head when he saw what appeared at first to be the beginning of a fine vapour trail over the Portland area – a trail such as any high-flying aircraft might make.

He very soon realised it was not a vapour trail because it did not grow in length or begin to spread out and disintegrate. Instead it came flashing down at an incredible speed until he could see that it was actually a curiously shaped craft. At a height of between two and three hundred feet it decelerated abruptly as if in response to a powerful reverse thrust, levelled off and remained hovering above the ground about four hundred yards away from where he lay. Now he could see it in detail.

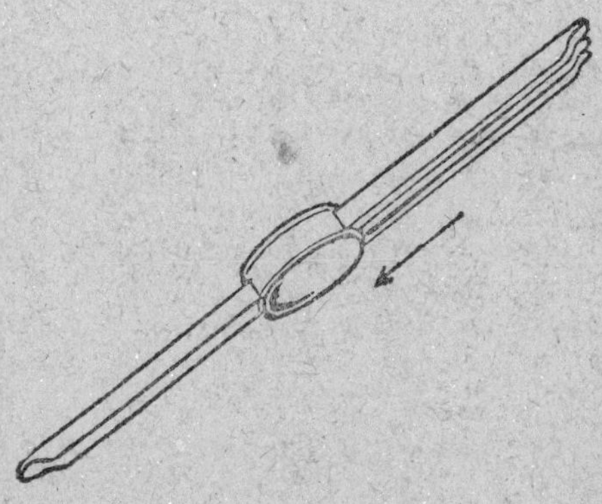

1. Arrival fuselage positions

There was a drum-like chamber amidships with four girder like 'fuselages' sprouting from it. As the thing had swooped down, coming in from over the sea, one of the fuselages pointed ahead and the other three trailed behind like the feathers of a bird's tail (see sketch 1). Then, as it hung in the sky, the trailing fuselages opened out like the spokes of a wheel equidistant from one another, forming a cross with the drum-shaped chamber in the middle.

While Mr Brooks watched, the craft slowly rotated ninety degrees in a clockwise direction and then remained motionless unaffected by the very strong wind (sketch 2). The craft seemed to be constructed of some translucent material. It had made no sound as it approached and remained silent throughout the time it was hovering equidistant between Winfrith Atomic Station and Portland Underwater Defence Station, and about a mile inland from the USAAF Communications Unit at Ringstead Bay.

The craft hovered for twenty-two minutes, then resumed its original shape with one fuselage pointing ahead (though not the same one) and the other three lined up behind, and a moment later it shot away at increasing speed to disappear high in the sky beyond Winfrith. In his report to the Ministry of Defence Mr Brooks said that although he had heard nothing the visit

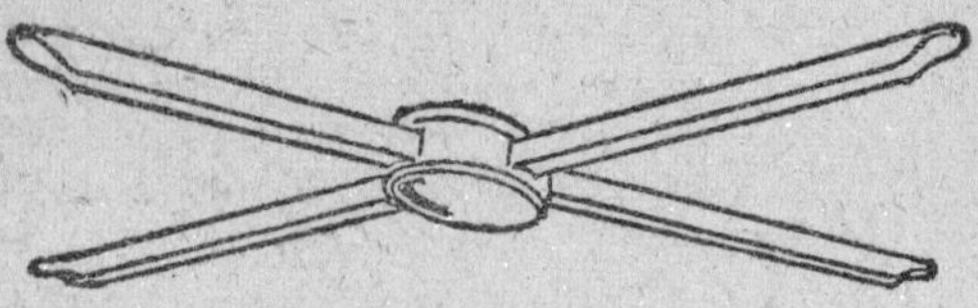

2. Hovering fuselage positions

of the craft had clearly affected one of his dogs, a twelve-year-old alsatian bitch called Tana. The animal, normally perfectly happy to be with him on the Downs, seemed very distraught and kept pawing at him as if urging him to leave the spot. She would take no notice of his orders to 'sit' though continuing to stay with him. The other dog, a dalmatian, had gone off hunting game.

When I met Mr Brooks some months after the sighting, I was impressed, as others have been, by his obvious sincerity and his genuine regret that nobody else in the area seemed to have seen the craft. The reason for this was not difficult to understand. When I walked on Moigne Downs with him to see the exact spot from which he claimed to have seen the UFO nothing impressed me so much as its immense loneliness. And this was a warm summer's day, whereas on the day of the sighting, although the sky had been clear, the weather had been cold and gusty.

Mr Brooks was in no doubt that he had seen an alien craft although he saw no movement indicating that anyone was aboard it. There were dark shadows suggesting grooves under each of the fuselages, he said, but he had seen no portholes or form of 'window' from which crew members could look out.

'When hovering, the craft looked about 175 feet in diameter,' he told me. 'I judged that from the length of a Comet 4 which is 110 feet long. I am used to looking at Comets. To begin with I was apprehensive, wondering if I had been spotted. It even crossed my mind that I might be captured and I planned, if there seemed any danger of that, to leave my walking stick in the ground as a clue to where I had been. But after a bit I felt easier, even content, and it has since occurred to me that the green anorak I was wearing may have camouflaged me.'

At first, Mr Brooks told me, he decided not to say anything about his experience. Other people claiming to have seen UFOs had run up against ridicule and the suspicion that they were a little barmy. On reflection, however, he felt he had a duty to say what he had seen, and if it was going to be reported, he felt he would be in a position to give as clear an account of the thing as anyone – possibly clearer. He did not know then that he would be the only person to report the UFO. But first he went back to his bungalow in the little village of Owermoigne and told his wife Christine about the experience. 'I have just seen one of those things,' he said, and got the reply: 'Oh, no!'

Afterwards, Mr Brooks told his story to the local vicar who, before taking orders, had been a senior police officer and who advised him to make the initial report to the Weymouth police. Mr Brooks also took the trouble to check with Winfrith to see if any odd effects had been noticed at the time, but nothing unusual had been reported and the American unit said much the same. But what was more disappointing was that nobody at all seemed to have shared his experience. At least if they had, they did not come forward, although the story was told on television and radio.

Not long afterwards Mr Brooks was interviewed by investigators from the Ministry of Defence who, after considering all the circumstances, came up with the explanation that all Mr Brooks had seen was a 'floater' or piece of cellular debris in his own eye. Since he had been lying down and *might* have fallen asleep, this could have triggered off a vivid dream. Was it not possible that the dog was simply worried by the fact that her master was lying down perfectly still and was anxious to get him on his feet again?

Such an explanation is certainly not devoid of common sense

but Mr Brooks is still convinced that he saw nothing less than a flying machine unlike any to be seen on earth. He reminded me of the story dating back to the time when jet air services across Africa started. An African village boy had been laughed to scorn for insisting that he had seen a strange craft passing overhead – until news of the service eventually reached the village.

'Before the Moigne Downs sighting,' he said, 'I was only mildly interested in unidentified flying objects but now I am convinced there is something to be investigated and the sooner we find out what is going on the better it will be.'

For his own part Mr Brooks has circulated an account of his sighting to flying saucer research organizations all over the world in the hope that he will obtain confirmation for the Moigne Downs sighting from someone else who may chance to see the same sort of craft.

Design engineer Mr R. H. B. Winder commenting in *Flying Saucer Review*, probably the most objective publication of its kind in the world, was clearly as impressed as I was by the integrity of Mr Brooks, but could offer no easy explanation to account for the shape of the craft. He wrote: 'I cannot at present recall any precedent, although I realize it could be associated with several of the "Flying Star" descriptions given by other witnesses around the same period. It is difficult to rationalize the four fuselages. They are certainly not aerodynamic, and it is unlikely that they have anything to do with propulsion. I say this because the central disc is quite saucer-like and, as we know very well, a disc of that size would alone be fully capable of the performance described.

'In fact one way of looking at the problem is to regard this object as a modification of a standard saucer for some special purpose sufficiently important to justify the obvious encumbrance. For example, if the craft were electrically or hydromagnetically driven, the regions of intense ionization or high magnetic field strength close to its centre would interfere with certain radio type transmitters or receivers and upset any magnetic instruments. The extensions might therefore have been devised to remove such instruments from those regions. However, that does not explain the use of four arms. We would not expect one to be used because it might upset the balance of the craft, but it is difficult to understand why two should not suffice and, indeed, eliminate the folding procedure which is presumably necessary to reduce drag during flight.'

Mr Winder, who has been studying UFO phenomena since 1952, clearly has no difficulty in accepting the notion that a craft *was* seen by Mr Brooks. In contrast it is interesting to see now a trio of investigators from the Defence Ministry approached the matter:

Dear Mr Brooks,

1 As promised at our meeting I am writing to let you know the conclusions we have reached on your report about the object you saw at Owermoigne on 26th October.

2 The information which you provided both in your written reports and our discussions has been most carefully checked. We have also examined all possible activities in the area which might have given rise to your sighting but have been unable to trace any other evidence of unusual or unauthorized aerial activity. In addition, in spite of the extensive local publicity on the television, radio and in the Press no corroborating reports have been received. Whilst it is true that the spot from which you made the observation is relatively remote, we did see some human activity during our walk to and from it last month; a farm worker on a tractor and a van on the road on the opposite hillside. It seems unlikely that an object, which you estimated as having an overall length of 150 feet, could have hovered above the horizon for twenty-two minutes, unnoticed by anyone else.

3 We do not doubt that the experience which you have described was a very vivid one, nor have we overlooked your long association with aviation. However, we are unable to agree with your conclusion that you saw a controlled flying vehicle of unique design and performance. I know this may seem to contradict you, but I am sure you will understand that the information you have given us is capable of other interpretations which we believe are the more likely explanation of what you saw.

4 The explanation is this. You have told us that on the morning of 26th October, 1967, you were walking with your dogs on Moigne Downs. There was a gale force wind blowing and you decided to shelter from it and at the same time to look for something unusual in the sky, that is to say, a bright

star which you hoped you might see in daylight. You first saw a contrail which was the normal vapour trail produced by a high flying aircraft, but this had no physical connection with the subsequent sequence of events. The next thing you saw was a vitreous floater – a piece of loose matter (a dead cell) floating in the fluid of the eyeball. Such objects appear as rods and/or discs, are present in most peoples' eyes and are more noticeable when one is looking at a brightly lit source of even colouring such as a clear sky. The fact that you had an eye injury some years ago, since repaired by corneal transplant, makes it possible that there may have been some larger floaters than usual. There are several similarities between the object you described and the floater, particularly its translucency and the slightly darker centre line of the rod-like components. The downward and transverse movement of the object is compatible with the natural movement of a floater when the eye is held stationary and the direction and speed of departure of the object match the movement of a floater when the eye is flicked upwards. However, it is unlikely that the floater would have remained stationary for as long as twenty-two minutes. But, you will recall that you had the impression that the sighting lasted for a much shorter period than the twenty-two minutes shown on your watch. It seems possible, therefore, that on lying down, after walking over rough country in a force eight gale you were feeling a little tired and you feel asleep or entered a near sleep state.

5 There had been a great deal of publicity in October about UFO sightings and this, the floater and the fact that you had been looking for an object in the sky could have triggered off a dream in which the floater took on the more elaborate form you have described. Your instant knowledge and certainty of its size and distance and intent are all suggestive of the immediate and inexplicable awareness which are characteristic of many dreams. The distress of your alsatian could be explained by her finding you in an unusual state, asleep in the open air, rather than by the presence of an unusual object.

6 I recognize that you may find our conclusions unsatisfactory but in the light of the information available to us, we must form our own judgment about the object you have described. As I have said, we have no other evidence of any

unusual aerial activity in Dorset that day nor, despite wide publicity, has any other witness come forward. While it would be intellectually arrogant to dispute the hypothesis that in the infinity of space, there could be other intelligent life, we have no proof of this. Neither have the reports of unidentified flying objects passed to us provided evidence that extra-terrestrial craft have visited earth. Our radar cover is such that we are also quite satisfied that there is no clandestine aerial activity over the United Kingdom under terrestrial control. With respect, your report does not give us cause to alter these conclusions.

7 Finally, I should like to thank you very much indeed for your extremely detailed and interesting report and for the kind welcome and whole-hearted co-operation you gave to Mr Dickison, Mr Cassie and myself when we visited you in February.

Yours sincerely,
L. Akhurst.

The investigating team were in fact Dr John Dickison, a Farnborough scientist, Mr Alec Cassie, an RAF psychologist and the writer Leslie Akhurst who belongs to the Ministry of Defence secretariat.

As an exercise in rationalization their findings could hardly be improved upon and who is to say they are not perfectly correct. Unfortunately there is only one man who is in a position to evaluate the explanation with any authority. Mr Brooks showed what he thought of it in a letter he wrote to Mr Akhurst on 28 April 1968. In the course of the letter he wrote: I propose to take your report by paragraph and comment.

Paragraph 2

1 Corroborative reports in the area were received. These were night sightings of 'star' and 'dart' shaped craft. Either format could be affected by the Moigne Downs UFO with its fuselage control.

2 On the day of your visit there was one farm worker on our side of the valley and one van passed along the far road on the other side. This confirms that the percentage of activity in such a large and remote area is so low that on the day of the sighting

it was more than possible that I was alone in the area. This has been the case in the previous eight months.

Paragraph 3

1 The report of any one person's experience can open interpretation permutations covering the range from frank disbelief to 'Establishment' oriented conclusions and I cannot but think that your contradiction of my interpretation of the very vivid experience, that you agree I had, must stem from the latter. Your paragraph 4 only strengthens this thought.

Paragraph 4

1 The 'con' trail mentioned was not a normal vapour trail as it disappeared almost at once and must have been the craft's angled reflection in the sun. Vapour trails, as we know, continue with the aircraft and produce lengthy 'streamer' effects.

2 The 'floater' theory (what an unfortunate choice of name) means: Mistake, Bloomer, in dictionary slang. Muscae volitantes, my specialist informs me, move upwards and downwards and, as the craft entered the vision circle at 030 deg., moved across descending to centre of vision, hovered for twenty-two minutes, then exited vision circle at 320 deg., this hardly conforms.

As my eyes were not stationary during the observation the chances of the exact similar shaped MV being present in both eyes at the exact same time can be discounted. The corneal implant of two years before had only improved the vision and MVs had not been noticeable in the eye concerned. I understand that rod-like MVs are exceedingly rare and seldom, if ever, linked.

3 In our discussion, my comment was not that my impression of the observation was shorter than the elapsed time but that after a period I had lost the feeling of time due to the intense interest and admiration I was feeling for the craft's construction and of its non-aggressive appearance.

4 I walk daily for around two hours over rough country in all Met conditions and wind forces. I do not stop for rest as I look upon this walk in the same way as I used to run each morning for exercise when at the office and, as for sleeping *en route* ... please! ! The fact that the gale was howling and

my alsatian was painfully clawing me to leave the spot was hardly conducive of 'dropping off'.

Paragraph 5

1 It is normally contended that dream 'triggers' are of more personal involvement than everyday news and I had not been particularly interested in the UFO 'splashes' at the time.

2 My instant knowledge, certainly of size, distance and intent are indeed suggestive of the immediate awareness of the existence of the craft.

3 The alsatian would not obey spoken or physical orders to remain still on the day and, on the two following days (with witnesses) at the site, showed distress which could only be attributable to having been pained or frightened at the craft's appearance. She could have received a high VHF signal.

Paragraph 6

1 In your Conclusions your disadvantage is, of course, that I was there at the time and any Investigation Commission can only work on the creditability of second hand report details combined with technical, medical and scientific assistance, so, with reciprocal respect, your conclusions have not given me cause to alter my opinion of the Moigne Downs UFO.

Although, at the start of this experience, I had no wish to become involved in the UFO story, I now find I am interested enough to be doing some thinktank work on this. May I suggest that 'Fatigue Mirages' and 'Ghostings' be given some 'lateral' thought by your department and, on completion of my studies, I will pass my results for discussion between us.

We should be happy to see you any time you are in this area. I enjoyed our meeting and, next time, who knows, the Moigne Downs UFO may give you the doubtful 'privilege' of seeing it. My best regards to John Dickison and Alec Cassie and, of course, to yourself.

Yours,

April 28 1968 Angus Brooks

If it does nothing else this letter clearly reveals the mind of a man who is normally pretty wide awake, a man who would be unlikely to fall asleep anywhere and then, on waking, fail to realize he *had* been asleep. What Mr Brooks claims to have seen over Moigne Downs presents a truly remarkable puzzle and one cannot help being impressed by the coincidence that he should describe what amounts to a Flying Cross seen in broad daylight.

There may, of course, be an explanation that nobody has thought of yet. But meanwhile, I suggest, the Moigne Downs sighting must be regarded as a 'genuine' UFO in the sense that it *was* in the sky and not simply in the eye of the beholder.

3

More of the Flap

Not the least of the curious events of October 1967 concerned Mr B. J. Collett, director of a transport business in Sussex who was driving a Ford transit bus from his home to deliver a consignment of titanium castings to Redditch near Birmingham. Mr Collett had got up before dawn and at 4.30 a.m. was driving along the A32 towards Reading. He had a clear level road fairly well illuminated by moonlight and was listening to Spanish music on the car radio. He had nothing to worry him; indeed he was looking forward to completing his journey in good time when the radio faded out, the car's headlights failed and the engine went dead on him. Mr Collett applied his brakes and got out of the driving seat to look under the bonnet.

For everything to go at once like that the battery must be at fault, he decided. Perhaps a lead had come adrift. But no. Both leads were intact and firmly connected to the terminals. Furthermore, as far as he could see, nothing else was wrong either: he checked fuses, plug leads and distributor without success and eventually decided to return to the driving seat and try the self-starter again.

While doing so he noticed a shadowy object outlined against the sky further up the road. It was not so obvious that it commanded his attention but he was nevertheless aware of it as he turned the ignition key . . . again without result. Wondering what to do Mr Collett sat for several minutes. When he next tried the ignition key the engine came vigorously to life, the lights came on and so did the radio.

Mr Collett let in the clutch and released the brakes. But about 400 yards along the road the car 'died' on him again and again he got out to look under the bonnet – for this time he was aware of the smell of electrical burning. It did not, however, appear to be coming from the vehicle. He straightened up, looked round once more and again noticed the looming object in the sky, about a hundred yards away.

Mr Collett did not connect its presence with his predicament. The thing was still not making a great impact on his mind, he says, but whatever it was it was *there* and he formed a clear impression of its shape and size. It was rather like a flattish ice cream cone sixty feet across the rim and about thirty feet from the curved upper surface to the point of the conical under structure.

Mr Collett says he watched it for several minutes trying to make up his mind about it and presently saw the thing glide silently away to the right and disappear over some trees. When it had gone he tried his ignition switch and found the vehicle all right again. It was an odd experience but he did not tell the story to the newspapers, not wishing to be involved in the saucer flap and thinking that no doubt there was a rational explanation. Besides, he realized, there were no witnesses to support his story. But the incident continued to puzzle him and a few days later he got in touch with Mr Charles Bowen, editor of *Flying Saucer Review*, who arranged for him to be interviewed by Dr Bernard Finch and Mr R. H. B. Winder.

The doctor who has been a saucer investigator for fifteen years questioned him closely and was impressed by Collett's sincerity. He learned that the motorist had had a feeling of tension which many people have experienced before a thunderstorm and that his eardrums had been popping – a sensation familiar to air travellers.

'Obviously,' the doctor reported, 'there must have been considerable air pressure changes in the vicinity of the object. When Mr Collett resumed his driving, he found that he had considerable difficulty in co-ordinating the movements of his hands and feet. It was as if he 'had to learn the movements of driving all over again', and that all involuntary movements had to be carried out with deliberation.

'These symptoms have occurred in other witnesses who have been near UFOs and one can only assume that the "Force Field" has interfered with the peripheral nerves and their connections in the spinal cord so that the reflex-arc has been temporarily "knocked out". In support of these findings we learned that Mr Collett later complained of a strange "tingling numbness and crawling feelings" at the end of his fingers – a very descriptive account of regenerating nerves . . .

'All in all, it appears that Mr Collett was affected by the periphery of a force field which we assume was contracted down to its minimum. The saucer was hovering, there was practically no glow nor sound, and we may assume the "engine" was obviously at low thrust. Had the engine been on full throttle it would have been a different kettle of fish. The saucer would have been surrounded by a brilliant violet glow, the force field would have extended outwards several hundred yards and Mr Collett would have been knocked unconscious, his skin being rendered erythematous.

'And when he recovered would he have been the same man? Would his cerebral neurones have acted as before? I doubt it. I suspect his memory and concentration would have been impaired, and the auditory and visual cortex recovering from its "stunning process" would begin to show various activities.

'For, as the peripheral nerves in recovering give rise to "tingling" so the auditory and visual cortex in recovering give rise to "sounds" and "visions" respectively. And as we have seen with previous witnesses there would be auditory and visual hallucinations.

'In all contact ground level sightings,' says the doctor, 'one must bear in mind the considerable side effects of the force field on the physiology of the human body.'

Mr Collett's experience brings to mind a similar sighting story, hallowed in saucer lore, which happened five years earlier and still remains unexplained in any rational way. It happened at 3.30 a.m. on 9 February 1962 when Mr Ronald Wildman of Luton, Bedfordshire, was starting out to deliver a new Vauxhall car to an address in Swansea. He was going at a comfortable forty miles an hour along the lonely Ivinghoe road at Aston Clinton, Buckinghamshire. The road curves a good deal and as Mr Wildman rounded one of the bends he saw a large whitish, metallic-looking object hovering above the roadway, about thirty feet up.

'It was oval shaped and white with black marks at regular intervals round it, which could have been portholes or air vents,' he said. 'It was about twenty to thirty feet above the ground and at least forty feet wide across – which in my estimation was fantastic.

'As soon as I came within twenty yards of it the power of my car changed, it dropped right down to twenty m.p.h. I changed down to second and put my foot flat on the accelerator – nothing happened.

'I had my headlights full on and although the engine lost revs the lights did not fade. The object, which was silent, kept ahead of me by approximately twenty feet for 200 yards, then started to come lower. It continued like this till it came to the end of the stretch. Then a white haze appeared round it, like a halo round the moon. It veered off to the right at a terrific speed and vanished; as it did so it brushed particles of frost from the tree tops on to my windscreen. It was definitely a solid object because the reflection of my headlights was thrown back from it.'

Mr Wildman told investigators who visited him at his home that until this incident he had been highly sceptical of flying saucers. They found no books or other literature on the subject at the house. It was unfortunate that there were no other witnesses of the saucer, but under the circumstances it is not really surprising. At that hour in the morning only people who have specific duties to attend to are normally abroad. But it is strongly in Mr Wildman's favour that he reported the incident to Aylesbury police station before continuing his journey. The police found him sober and sensible and thought he was telling the truth as he knew it.

As has happened on many occasions before and since, there was no official inquiry into the matter. The Air Ministry, according to a *Daily Telegraph* report, were of the opinion that what Wildman had seen was nothing more than a low cloud lit up by his headlights, but even the most sceptical reader must find this an unsatisfactory explanation. Mr Wildman was accustomed to night driving and is surely entitled to be accepted as a man who can recognize a cloud when he sees one. Clouds do not normally have 'portholes or vents' round the rim; nor do they brush frost particles from tree tops as they move away – a detail in Mr Wildman's narrative which has a remarkable ring of truth. It is certainly not the sort of thing that the average person would imagine. On this evidence alone (albeit hearsay evidence) one is inclined to say that whatever Wildman saw it certainly was not a cloud. As this was the only rational explanation offered by anyone at the time one is faced with the alternatives that either Mr Wildman was lying about the whole episode or that he was hallucinated. It seems unlikely he was lying. What would be the point? And why would he risk trouble with the police? So perhaps he suffered an hallucination. I have not met the man but several friends of mine have and say they found him alert and intelligent, a man doing a job which he would be unlikely to hold down if he were anything but a calm and reasonable person – very like Mr Collett.

In my opinion both men are reliable witnesses, telling the truth. What they saw may still be in dispute, a reasonable explanation in terrestrial terms may yet be forthcoming, but there is little doubt in my mind they saw *something* – just as did two schoolgirls walking near Dunoon, Argyllshire, in September 1959.

The girls – fourteen-year-old Patricia Murchison and thirteen-year-old Linda McCulloch – arrived home one evening frightened to the point of hysteria by what they had experienced. Police who spoke to them were satisfied that they were telling the truth and luckily, this time, it turned out that there were witnesses.

The girls said they had gone for an evening walk to Sandbank about two miles from Dunoon and on their way back along the high road they had seen two UFOs in the sky. They described the UFOs as 'black and white and round, and tapering to a point at the bottom' – a description which is not far off those given by Collett and Wildman. Neither of the girls was able to give specific details but Patricia said emphatically: 'They were flying saucers. They definitely were. We were walking along the road when we suddenly noticed the two things in the sky. We were scared. We ran into a field at Ardnadam Farm and tried to hide. But they came down until they were just above the telegraph poles. We got up and moved but they followed. We were terrified. We ran into a ditch to hide and they hovered above us. We tried to stop cars on the road but none would stop.'

Eventually one did stop however and a man and woman got out: Mr Henry English of Paisley who was on holiday with his wife at a nearby caravan site. One of the girls asked him: 'Can you see anything up there?'

Mr English looked at the sky. 'There were two things floating about,' he said later. 'I got scared myself. They were round and big – just above us. It wasn't a mirage. I'll swear they were flying saucers.'

In a later report on the incident, Linda said of the UFOs: 'They went round and round. Sometimes they went away and then they came back again. There was no noise from them. I've never been so scared in my life.'

The Dunoon saucers created a stir at the time and were then forgotten. Again there was no official investigation although the Air Ministry said emphatically that no conventional aircraft, which might have been mistaken for saucers, were around at the time. There is no question that the girls were genuinely and severely frightened – but of what? Though only in their early teens they were old enough to recognize commonplace aircraft – had commonplace aircraft behaved in that mysteriously inquisitive manner.

The saucer flap in 1967 was distinguished if for nothing else by the fact that so many sightings were reported by policemen. Policemen can make mistakes like anyone else but at least they are trained observers and not the class of people one would suspect of suffering from hallucinations.

The sighting reported by PC Colin Perks in March 1966 is a case in point. PC Perks was patrolling the streets of Wilmslow, Cheshire, at dawn in February of that year when he saw, so he claims, an immense UFO sailing through the sky not more than a hundred yards from where he stood in Alderley Road. It was about thirty feet in diameter and as bulky as a double-decker bus, he said.

He reported: 'There was an eerie, greenish-grey glow in the sky. Then I picked out an object about thirty feet long built up in three sections with the top looking like a dustbin lid. It gave off a high-pitched whine.'

The policeman added: 'I was paralyzed. I just couldn't believe it.' He watched the object for fully five minutes until it disappeared.

And in May that year PC Donald Cameron made out a report claiming to have spotted no less than six UFOs. PC Cameron was on sick leave at his home in Chilton Road, St Helens, Lancs. He and his wife were looking out of the window when they saw the UFOs about a mile away travelling south-east.

'We could see them quite clearly,' he said, 'although it was a dull day. They were white and glowing. One was bigger than the others with a cup-shaped dome – obviously the mother ship. The others were oval.'

Police were involved also in a remarkable sighting in Southampton in September 1966. It had started with a 999 call from Mr John Dack of Coxford Road, Southampton, who noticed a UFO hanging motionless in the sky over the city. He told the police: 'You're not going to believe this, but there is a bright light in the sky and it keeps giving off purple flashes.'

At that point the police did not believe him but a Z-car was ordered to go and investigate. Then, minutes later, the car crew radioed to their headquarters: 'He's right. There is an object in the sky to the west and remaining still. It keeps flashing red, white and blue lights and dropping coloured flares. There's no sound of an engine and it does not appear to be an aircraft.'

Calls were put through to Eastleigh Airport and Southampton University Air Squadron but neither of them could offer an explanation. They were emphatic that there were no aircraft in the area. Inquiries were also made to the Southern Meteorological Centre from which came the reply that the experts could not suggest any natural phenomena to account for the sightings.

The mysterious object vanished after making off at great speed towards Eastleigh and has remained unexplained ever since – just like the 'dustbin lid' seen by PC Perks and the formation of oval-shaped things reported by PC Cameron.

No less mysterious was the mushroom-shaped object which a thirteen-year-old schoolboy claimed to have seen being chased by RAF Lightning jets over Winchester one Friday afternoon during the October flap. Timothy Robinson, along with his parents and other members of the family, were having a cup of tea after a late lunch at their home in Pitts Corner, Winchester, when they were startled by the roar of jet aircraft overhead. The time was 2.20 p.m. The noise was so loud that Timothy's father, who teaches electrical engineering at Southampton College of Technology, cried out: 'What on earth's that?' and ran to the front door while the boy made for the french windows opening on to the back garden.

When I telephoned the family next morning, Timothy told me: 'I saw the Lightnings go over at about four times the height of the house. There were two of them. I recognized them by their swept-back wings. It wasn't difficult because I make model aircraft.'

He had spotted the second Lightning first and then looked ahead to see the leading one. But that was not all, for still further ahead was a black mushroom-shaped object streaking away in the sky.

'It was hanging tail down, not spinning, but going at a tremendous speed,' Timothy said. 'It was going west, then abruptly changed direction to north-west and disappeared into a cloud, climbing steeply. It looked as if the aircraft were banking to follow it but were outmanoeuvred.'

From the front door, the boy's father had not been able to see even the aircraft and when he dashed upstairs to look out of a back bedroom window it was too late to catch sight of them. 'However, I am satisfied my son saw something,' he told me. 'He came in and said it was a couple of Lightnings chasing a flying saucer.'

It is arguable, of course, that in the excitement of the moment the boy was mistaken in what he saw. The mushroom-shaped object might have been a curious cloud formation, the distorted shadow of an aircraft or a balloon. But what seems beyond doubt is that aircraft, probably Lightnings, did go over the house. Yet the Ministry of Defence were unable to account for the presence of Lightnings over Winchester at that time. They denied emphatically that Lightnings had taken off on any defence operation and were even unable to explain the presence of *any* aircraft. The mystery began and ended with the roar of low-flying jets that disturbed the Robinson family at their tea.

What it was all about still remains unclear; but as far as the mushroom-shaped object is concerned I can only say that Timothy Robinson seemed to me a sensible, level-headed boy with above average ability as an aeroplane spotter. What he claims to have seen leaves us with yet another unexplained UFO sighting.

4
Early Days

UFOs are not peculiar to the post-war era. People have been seeing odd things in the sky throughout recorded history. As far back as 1646, for example, a book was published called *Strange Signes from Heaven,* which recorded sightings of many phenomena which would well come under the general heading of flying saucers, and even in the Bible there are references suggesting that ancient people were puzzled by them.

One of the most sensational 'saucers' of more modern times was seen over London in November 1882 and among qualified observers to notice it was Mr Walter Maunder, a Greenwich astronomer. It was not until 1916, however, that Mr Maunder published an account of the sighting in *The Observatory*, in response to a request from the Royal Astronomical Society to describe the most remarkable thing he had ever seen in the course of many years sky gazing.

He said that just after sunset on 17 November 1882, he was looking across London from the roof of Greenwich Observatory, when: 'A great circular disc of greenish light suddenly appeared down in the East-North-East as though it had just risen, and moved across the sky, as smoothly and steadily as the sun, moon, stars and planets move, but nearly a thousand times as quickly. The circularity of its shape was merely the effect of fore-shortening, for as it moved it lengthened out, and when it crossed the meridian and passed just above the moon its form was almost that of a very elongated ellipse, and various observers spoke of it as "cigar-shaped" or "like a torpedo" . . .'

The object was seen by hundreds of people all over Britain and even on the Continent, and pretty accurate figures were obtained for its size and speed. It was more than a hundred miles above the earth, moving at about ten miles a second and must have been at least fifty miles long. Nobody in those days had been able to give an adequate explanation for it but I doubt whether many present-day scientists would be unduly puzzled. The object had appeared at the time of a violent magnetic storm and was almost certainly part of an auroral display caused by charged particles from the sun plunging into the earth's atmosphere and lighting it up like a neon tube.

A beam of particles tracking across the country would have created what appeared to be a solid object moving at speed; and this is borne out by the fact that when the beam had spent its force the mysterious object broke up over the Continent like a cloud being torn to pieces by upper atmosphere gales.

Flying saucers, in the sense that many people regard them today, did not come into their own until 24 June 1947. On that day, Kenneth Arnold, an American businessman from Idaho was making a routine business trip to Washington in a private plane. The journey took him parallel with a range of snow-capped mountains and he was startled to see a formation of strange objects swerving in and out of the mountain peaks. Never having seen anything like them before he reported the experience as soon as he reached his destination. He described the objects as 'a chain of saucer-like things'.

At first Mr Arnold's report was not taken too seriously but the word 'saucer' captured public imagination. Reports of other flying saucers were soon coming in from all over the United States and indeed from all over the world.

What they were nobody could say and nobody knows for certain to this day. But the most attractive theory was that they were flying machines piloted by strange visitors from outer space. Headlines flared. 'IS ANOTHER WORLD WATCHING US? they demanded. Cartoonists worked overtime and hoaxers rampaged the country.

Then something happened that made people wonder if it was all such a joke after all. Flying saucers suddenly became a world mystery and even a world menace. The happening was the appearance of a UFO over Godman Field, Fort Knox, on 7 January 1948 – a portentous day for all who were stationed there at the time.

The day had begun quite normally and cheerfully with routine flight training in clear sunny weather. Nobody was thinking about flying saucers. But that was before the alarm was raised, before the jangling chorus of phone bells sounded and harsh radio instructions crackled from Godman tower, before the men of Fort Knox ran into the open and stood looking up at the sky with shaded eyes.

Up there, at the hazy limit of visibility, was something later described as 'a huge ice cream cone topped with red.'

Four National Guard P-51 planes roared off the tarmac to investigate, and from one of them as it dwindled into the sky came back the tense voice of Captain Thomas Mantell of the United States Air Force. 'There it is! Twelve o'clock high. It looks metallic . . . a tremendous size.'

None of the other pilots had it in sight, and presently Captain Mantell radioed that the thing was climbing rapidly. 'I'm going to follow it up to 20,000 feet,' he said. 'If I'm no closer I'll abandon chase.'

On the ground they waited. They tried calling him back, but nothing more was heard from Captain Mantell and nothing was seen until his broken body was recovered from the wreckage of the plane which crashed a few miles away. Meanwhile the 'cone', still unseen by the other pilots, had disappeared. And just what happened up there is still in doubt; but there is a persistent belief in some quarters that Mantell got too close, saw too much and was destroyed by some power unknown on earth.

The incident has a fundamental place in the whole flying saucer mystery. Indeed it might be argued that had Mantell not died the saucers would have died instead, for his death occurred at a time when interest in flying saucers was beginning to flag. As it was, it boosted the mystery into a new phase in which every new sighting would stir up the old excitement.

Opponents of the notion that flying saucers are craft from outer space insisted that Mantell was not shot down by a Martian death-ray but blacked out through lack of oxygen and crashed without regaining consciousness. And the UFO he was chasing? It might have been a 'skyhook' balloon such as was used to study cosmic rays – later whipped away in a high altitude gale. Or it might have been a 'mock sun' caused by ice crystals in cirrus clouds which lay higher than Mantell's plane could reach. But there was no clue to be found in the wreckage and to this day nobody knows the answer for sure.

While on the subject, however, it is interesting to recall that a giant cone-shaped object was observed at a height of about 15,000 feet above Brixham, Devon, at noon on 28 April 1967.

Scores of people along the Devon coast telephoned police stations to ask about the object which, according to one newspaper, was slowly revolving.

The object was also observed by coastguards using high-powered glasses, the newspaper said, and as it turned some sort of door could be seen in its side.

Observers also claimed that they had seen an aeroplane approach, fly round the cone and then make off again as the cone began to climb higher into the sky, eventually disappearing in cloud at about 20,000 feet. It really looked as though, this time, Britain had had a sighting which would pass every test required of the sceptics. Apart from the fact that there were numerous independent witnesses on the ground, somebody must have got a close-up view of the UFO. Aircraft do not fly round objects that are not there.

And if an aircraft were involved, it had to come from a near-by base, the pilot would have reported the sighting and presumably the report would find its way to the Ministry of Defence. In fact, according to the newspaper, a report was forwarded to the Ministry by the RAF at Plymouth. However, when the Ministry were asked about it they at first denied having received the report. Later a Ministry spokesman admitted: 'Further inquiries reveal that we did receive a report but somehow it was not logged.'

What the report said was not disclosed but did not appear to have moved the Ministry unduly for the spokesman added: 'We can only suggest that the object may have been a reflection of car headlights or some sort of meteorological phenomenon. I cannot comment further.'

When this reaction was made known to a senior RAF controller at Plymouth his reply was: 'We reported all the details. I cannot tell you where the aircraft came from and you will have a job to get anyone to admit that one was sent up. I understand the UFO was also tracked by radar.'

At the coastguard station at Berry Head, Brixham, the chief officer Harry Johnson said: 'It's just laughable for anyone to suggest to a body of highly trained observers that this was the reflection of car headlights. It was midday. The object was obviously made of something highly polished and reflected the sunlight almost like a star.'

Coastguard Brian Jenkins said: 'I was able to make a

detailed drawing of it which I showed to an air vice-marshal who called at the station a few days later. His only comment was "Most interesting".'

All the remarks quoted above in connection with the Brixham sighting have been taken from newspaper reports published at the time and the possibility of errors affecting the sense of what was actually said has to be considered, but there can be little doubt that the 'cone' startled many people and contained features by no means common to all UFO sightings.

The notion that the 'cone' could have been the reflection of car headlights (if the reporting on this point is strictly accurate) is absurd. Who would have switched on headlights at midday? And even if this were the case it is unlikely that the light beams, which would have had to be uptilted at a steep angle, would have carried up to 20,000 feet! As for the alternative that 'some sort of meteorological phenomenon' was responsible, this will hardly do either. One needs to know precisely what sort of phenomenon was in mind.

However, the Brixham sighting is not listed as unexplained, although the Defence Ministry say that it was reported too late for a thorough investigation. It was not tracked by radar. The Ministry is nevertheless satisfied that the 'cone' was nothing more than a high altitude balloon. As for a door opening in it and an aircraft flying round the object, this is officially put down to exaggeration on the part of some over-excited observer.

Well, it could be . . . But one cannot help feeling an opportunity was lost here, an opportunity to get really to grips with the UFO mystery and either expose it by means of photographs showing the 'cone' to be a balloon or to produce photographic evidence that it was something else – something perhaps requiring further investigation.

As it is, a good many people remain uncertain what to believe and may be forgiven for suspecting that officialdom clamped down on the subject. This is the view that many American people take about the Mantell UFO which is also officially classed as a balloon.

The first time that a British saucer sighting got official recognition (of a kind) was in November 1953. The case became known as the West Malling incident and was brought to the attention of the House of Commons.

At 10 a.m. on 3 November 1953, two members of the Royal Air Force, Flying Officer G. Smythe and Flying Officer T. S. Johnson were up in a two seater Vampire Jet fighter at about 20,000 feet. They saw an object which appeared at first as a stationary light. It was very bright. They could not determine the height but estimated that it was above 20,000 feet.

After they had observed it for a few seconds it began to move and shot above their aircraft at a very high speed. Although it was in sight for barely thirty seconds they had a good enough look at it to make out that it was perfectly circular. When they landed they reported the sighting to the West Malling Station Commander Group Captain P. H. Hanley, who sent the details to the headquarters at Fighter Command.

The two men were later questioned for more than two hours but it was a confidential interview and the details were never generally reported. The then Parliamentary Secretary to the Defence Ministry, when questioned about the West Malling incident in the Commons, said no more than that meteorological balloons were flying at the time. He added, amidst laughter, that there was nothing peculiar about the occurrences and an MP got another laugh by remarking that the West Malling incident could therefore be regarded as 'all ballooney'.

Nothing was said about the high speed at which the object moved, nor did anyone seem surprised that trained airmen, who must have seen many a balloon in flight, should have been mistaken about this one and thought it was something else. John Rowland in *Mysteries of Science** comments: 'The object, whatever it was, was, in fact very unlikely to have been a balloon; it is in the last degree unlikely that there was, even at a great height, a sudden gust of wind which would take a balloon out of sight in thirty seconds.'

And perhaps this is the place to recall also the famous Coniston sighting of a few months later and the photograph taken by a boy, Stephen Darbishire, a keen amateur photographer, who was walking in the Coniston area of the Lake District with his cousin, Adrian Meyer.

The date was 15 February 1954. Stephen, who had his camera with him, and his cousin were walking in the vicinity

* Neville Spearman Ltd

of a hill known as Coniston Old Man when they saw a curious object hovering above the hilltop. Both were excited about it and Stephen managed to get some pictures. They were not very good as, in his hurry, Stephen did not focus the camera very well, but one of his pictures clearly showed the outline of a UFO which conformed remarkably well with similar photographs alleged to have been taken in America.

To quote Rowland again: 'Stephen Darbishire is stated by everyone who has met him to be a completely reliable witness, and not the kind of boy who would be likely to make up such a story, just for the sake of the notoriety which would follow.

'In any event, a boy who was clever enough to fake the pictures obtained, would clearly not be the sort of boy whose statements would inspire confidence. The faker (if as young as Stephen Darbishire in 1954) is likely to give himself away when he is interviewed. And all those who met Stephen are agreed that he was a quiet, modest boy, and not at all the type to tell a tall story for the sake of making himself well known.'

About the time of the Coniston photograph I was invited to join a small group of newspapermen and scientists to watch a coloured film of UFOs taken from an aircraft which was flying above the clouds to photograph an eclipse of the sun. We sat on an assortment of office chairs in a darkened upper room in the West End of London, and the film which lasted only a few seconds was flashed on a wall screen.

The film was shown by an official of a Norwegian airline who said it had been shot from one of three Norwegian aircraft on the eclipse flight and that among the passengers were General Jorgenson, Commander-in-Chief of the Royal Norwegian Air Force, and members of the Royal Norwegian Astronomical Society.

The 'saucers' swooped into view above a frothing sea of white cloud 15,000 feet up and sped along the horizon like a pair of silver spotlights, keeping an even distance, one slightly above the other. They moved across the screen in an uptilted manner, then suddenly levelled off and vanished into the distance.

What happened aboard the aircraft at the time was told to me by Mr Ernest Graham of the Swedish Travel Agency who had been on the flight.

The sighting had taken place high above the clouds between Oslo and Stavanger, he said. After filming the eclipse with its fiery corona the scientists were returning to base when someone shouted: 'Look!' and pointed out at the brightening horizon. Someone else shouted: 'Binoculars! Has anyone brought binoculars?' But nobody had.

All the passengers and crew were now peering at the lights on the horizon which appeared as two silver discs. Then Mr Johnny Bjornylf, chief cameraman aboard the plane, swung his camera on to the skyline. The objects were in view for about half a minute, Mr Graham told me. They were between fifteen and twenty miles away and appeared to have a metallic glint.

'They must have been of enormous size,' he went on, 'and seemed to be solid. We could also see a rotary movement as they levelled off and dwindled out of sight. They could not have been reflections on glass because we had the windows out for the cameras and the plane was still in the shadow of the moon. Moreover they were too firm in outline to be clouds and were too obviously manoeuvrable.'

The UFOs were seen by fifty people who afterwards wrote reports about the sighting but there was no public announcement that anything other than the eclipse had been observed and after the film had been developed the 'saucer' sequence was cut out. It was not until eighteen months later that pressmen were allowed to see the 'censored' strip.

Nowadays such a precaution against publicity would seem absurd, but it should be remembered that saucers had become rather a touchy subject among orthodox scientists. If they could not laugh at them they preferred to ignore the whole subject. On this occasion, I understand, it was feared that the 'saucers' would bring ridicule on a serious scientific expedition.

I think, indeed, that this illustrates very strongly the extraordinary stand taken by orthodox science against the UFO phenomena. The Norwegian scientists apparently had no interest in the saucer pictures at all, apart from documenting the sighting. Yet, for all they could have known then, they might have photographed something of far greater importance than the eclipse. I remember, however, what Lord Dowding, former Air Chief Marshal, and head of Fighter Command during the Battle of Britain, said at the film show in London.

'The objects did not look like anything else except what one imagines flying saucers to look like,' he told me. 'I believe absolutely in the existence of flying saucers.'

Arthur C. Clarke, the science fiction writer and a man of great imagination, took, however, a much more doubtful view. 'I find it difficult to believe the shots were not taken through a window,' he said, 'perhaps in the heat of the moment, so that the objects were caused by reflections of light from somewhere in the aircraft. There was something on the screen that looked like the outline of a window to me. But there was obviously no deliberate faking.'

At the time I was more than a little inclined to agree with him. In fact a fine old argument developed between those who were convinced they had seen a film of flying saucers and those of us who were convinced that we had seen nothing of the sort. But again the matter has not been satisfactorily resolved.

Although many hundreds of saucer sightings had been reported from America for more than twenty years, and although there had been 'flaps' in Europe, Australia and Japan, it seemed that the phenomena were making no impact at all on the Soviet Union. And to many people no doubt this was significant. The Russians were far too sensible to concern themselves with nonsense of this sort! So it came as a surprise to learn, not long after the wave of sightings in Britain around October 1967, that they were just as puzzled over UFOs as the rest of the world.

Unidentified flying objects, said *Soviet Weekly*, published in London, were now so firmly established as a problem that an international effort was needed to solve it. Nor, it appeared, was this the newspaper's own view. The opinion was that of Professor Felix Zigel of Moscow's Institute of Aviation.

'It is not ruled out,' he was quoted as saying, 'that the solution could lead to some radical re-thinking . . .' which for a Russian spokesman was tantamount to going out on a limb. But in justification of the remark the newspaper added that a committee of scientists and other specialists had been established to make a systematic study of two hundred sighting reports. A preliminary analysis had, in fact, already been made and had led the committee to feel that the matter deserved thorough investigation.

The Soviet Union, it was disclosed, had even had its quota of sightings during the summer of 1967, only instead of flying crosses, catherine wheels and aerial cigars the Russians had seen glowing crescents in the sky. Reports of these had come not only from private individuals but from the Mountain Astronomical Station near Kislovodsk and an astronomical observatory in Kazan.

'The most characteristic type of UFO,' said *Soviet Weekly*, 'is a luminous orange-coloured crescent with a diameter of fifteen to twenty feet of arc, flying with its outward bend first. Its surface is reported only a little less luminous than that of the moon. The horns of the crescent throw out jets, sometimes with sparks. The outer contour of the crescent is sharp and the inner contour blurred and wavy.'

Sometimes, it was stated, the crescent was seen moving ahead of a bright flaming disc. At other times it was preceded and flanked by what looked like first-magnitude stars, which kept a constant distance from it. Kazan astronomers, who had observed crescents from two points simultaneously had estimated that the diameter of some of the crescent-shaped UFOs was between five hundred and six hundred metres and had judged their speed to be five kilometres a second.

'Assuming that the crescent is a shock wave,' said *Soviet Weekly*, 'the UFOs must fly at altitudes of between thirty and sixty-five miles. Such objects could not have been made by man. They are definitely not sputniks or space rockets.'

Among other sightings which, it was understood, the Soviet committee were looking into, was one reported by V. I. Duginov, director of the Khersov Hydro-meteorological School who claimed to have seen, while waiting at a bus stop, along with fifty other people, a glowing disc about one-third the sun's diameter travelling slowly eastwards. Yet another report had come from Latvian astronomers Robert Vitolniek, Jan Melderis and Esmeralda Vitolniek who were studying cloud formations from an observatory at Ogra on 26 July 1965. In the gathering dusk they had spotted an unusually bright star slowly moving westwards. With the help of binoculars they had been able to examine it in more detail and had observed that it had the shape of a disc thickened in the middle like a lens and with a 'ball' at the central point. In addition there were three other balls revolving round the perimeter.

The astronomers reckoned the disc was one hundred metres across. They had watched it for nearly twenty minutes, after which the balls appeared to take off from the disc and disappear while the disc itself dwindled until it also was lost to sight.

The Soviet UFO reports also included one from the navigator of an aircraft of Russia's polar aviation service dating back to 1956. The navigator, V. I. Akkuratov, had reported seeing a UFO over Greenland, rapidly closing in on the aircraft from the port side. This again had resembled a lens – with wavy, pulsating edges.

'To avoid collision with it,' Akkuratov had said, 'we dived back into the clouds. After forty minutes of flight in the direction of Medvezhi Island, the clouds suddenly receded and as we got into clear sky we noticed again the same flying object to port. We changed course sharply and began to approach it. In response, the UFO also changed course and flew parallel to us at a speed equal to our own.'

After nearly twenty minutes the UFO had suddenly shot ahead of the aircraft and disappeared into the blue. The aircraft crew had noticed neither superstructure nor portholes on the disc to indicate that it was piloted. 'There was neither a gas jet nor a vapour trail,' added Akkuratov, 'and the speed of its departure was so great that the whole phenomenon seemed something supernatural.'

According to Professor Zigel, said *Soviet Weekly*, the UFO phenomenon was real and could not be identified with any known natural phenomenon – with, for example, the anomalous optical phenomena in the earth's atmosphere. He had stated: 'Quite a number of UFOs have been observed over the USSR, and it is noteworthy that the UFO forms observed here fit into the classification of these objects accepted in the West, in the USA in particular.

'It is safe to claim that the UFO problem has assumed a global character and therefore calls for a global research. International scientific co-operation in the solution of this problem would long have become a reality, had not sensationalism and irresponsible anti-scientific assertions about "flying saucers" interfered with it.

'I have a profound respect for the efforts of such well-known American scientists as Professors Hynek and McDonald who are vigorously and with good reason trying to attract the attention of America's scientific public to the UFO problem. Unfortunately, certain scientists, both in the Soviet Union and in the United States, deny the very existence of the problem instead of helping to solve it.'

5
Why Warminster?

No town in Britain, possibly in the world, is more identified with the UFO mystery than the town of Warminster in Wiltshire. People interested in UFOs come from far and wide, especially when there is a 'flap' on, in the hope of seeing something strange in the skies over Warminster; and although they may go away disappointed, back they come again as soon as it is rumoured that the saucers are flying again.

If I myself have ever seen a UFO (and I am not sure that I have not) it was at Warminster on the night of Monday, 13 May 1968. But the details can wait for the time being. It is more important at this point to consider what took me to the town in the first place and why Warminster should feature so prominently on the UFO map.

There are few towns in Britain, or elsewhere, which I have visited in a lifetime of tracking down newspaper stories at home and abroad which has a more mysterious, not to say sinister atmosphere. The very name Warminster sounds vaguely horrific, hinting at an insubstantial clash of good and evil going on yesterday, today and evermore. It was here the invading Romans lived in a state of uneasy truce with the conquered Britons. It was here that King Alfred secretly assembled his armies for a final assault on the Danes in the great battle of Ethandunc.

And in more recent times Warminster was the meeting place of people from all over Britain, the place where coach roads came together and inns were built to accommodate travellers overnight. Some of those inns are still standing today and give you a strong feeling that spirits of the past are astir in them.

Today, the local guide book tells you, Warminster is still a county town of importance. It has long since lost its old-time cloth industry but has made up for that by adding a score of other industries and crafts. Paint, furniture, shoe components, gloves and greeting cards are produced here, whilst egg packing, light engineering, malting and barley research and, somewhat surprisingly, banana ripening are among local industrial activities. Warminster has also become an important military centre with the establishment of the School of Infantry and Workshops of the Royal Electrical and Mechanical Engineers. But the name Warminster has no connotation with actual belligerence. It is said to be derived from an ancient nunnery on the banks of the River Guere or Were and at the time of the Doomsday Survey was known as Guermestre. A later reference about AD 900 gives the name as Worgemynster.

When I arrived in Warminster the sky was heavily overcast and there were frequent showers. I had been there before but so long ago that I had forgotten what the town looked like. Even now nothing seemed to strike a chord of memory. I had arranged to meet a man whose knowledge of Warminster, its history and its mystery, should be unrivalled in the district. Arthur Shuttlewood is a local newspaper reporter and correspondent for Fleet Street but what interested me most was that he had published a graphic account of seeing a UFO for himself. In fact, I doubt whether any journalist in Britain has investigated more reports of UFO sightings than he has or has become personally interested to the same extent. Shuttlewood is a tall ex-guardsman who has lived and worked in and around Warminster for more than twenty years. I liked him immediately and although we met as strangers we sat down and talked over lunch for three hours without a moment's uneasiness. It was all about the strange noises said to have been heard by townspeople, weird crackling noises and thunderous rattlings as if roofs were being clawed apart; of huge cigar-shaped objects appearing overhead and (on one occasion) what looked like twin red-hot pokers hanging from the sky; of dazzling lights and 'balls of fire' said to have paralysed their beholders and brought motor vehicles inexplicably to a halt; of a remarkable photograph submitted to the *Warminster Journal* by Gordon Faulkner, a young factory worker and later published in the *Daily Mirror* of a UFO rather like a child's spinning top which he claimed to have seen and snapped from the back door of his home on 29 August 1965; of strange phone calls and an even stranger visitor to Shuttlewood's flat in the centre of the town.

It was about the time of the photograph that Shuttlewood

began to take a serious interest in the UFO mystery. He had been involved in it ever since, he said, but it was not until he had actually seen a UFO for himself that his attitude changed from one of simply investigating the facts to personally believing that there must be more to the mystery than appeared on the surface.

Journalists are often accused (quite wrongly as a rule) of mere sensationalism. Certainly if you have a story to write you try to make the most of it. Nobody wants to read a dull story. But the facts, as far as you can gather them, have to be there in the first place. And most journalists are pretty cynical people, not easily tricked by liars or hoodwinked by hoaxers, and my impression of Arthur Shuttlewood was that he would not 'go overboard' for a story and conveniently overlook the necessity to test the facts. He would certainly not *invent* a story. So what about the UFO he was personally prepared to vouch for?

It happened, he told me, at 3.42 p.m. on Tuesday, 28 September 1965. Shuttlewood had been working on a newspaper story in the sitting-room of his flat. Presently he left the room to go upstairs for a notebook and on reaching the landing he happened to glance out of a back window. What he saw kept him rooted to the spot. Sailing across the distant sky was a huge cigar-shaped object of gleaming white and amber, moving majestically from right to left.

'Suddenly I realized what I was looking at and rushed to get my movie camera,' he told me. 'But as I trained the camera on the sky it seemed to jump in my hands and I felt needling pains shoot up my left arm and the side of my face.'

However he managed to take several shots before the UFO entered a heavy belt of white cloud coming from the opposite direction. Camera poised he waited for the UFO to appear again but it did not simply emerge from the cloud. When he saw it again it was more than three miles along its course – a distance travelled in as many seconds!

It was receding so fast now that in a few more seconds it had dwindled to little more than a speck and, had he not been looking for it, Shuttlewood reckons, he would not have seen it at all. After it had disappeared from view he found that his face was twitching and his left eye watering. The twitching wore off pretty soon but he was left with a semi-paralyzed left hand for two days and his eye continued to trouble him for several weeks.

Unfortunately nobody else was in the house at the time of this sighting. Shuttlewood told me he had in fact stamped on the floor to warn his wife whom he thought was working in the kitchen below the landing, but he discovered later that she was out shopping. In fact nobody else in the whole of Warminster came forward to say they had seen a UFO that afternoon but this, he says, was probably because the thing was journeying mostly over waste ground outside the populated area of the town. Apart from this, seen from underneath it would probably have resembled a large dense, white cloud.

To begin with Shuttlewood was not bothered by the lack of witnesses to support his story. He had the camera. The film when developed would show precisely what he had seen. But unhappily the film did nothing of the kind. Something had happened to it (remember that jumping?) to cause the film to come adrift from the winding spool and get itself tangled up ineffectively away from the view finder. Except for what appeared to be some scorch marks there was nothing on the vital section of the film when he had it developed.

Now it is easy to be cynical about a story like this. Funny that nobody else saw the thing. Funny that Shuttlewood just happened to go upstairs at the time it was passing his window. Funny that he thought his wife was on the premises when she was out shopping. Funnier still that the movie camera should happen to go wrong at just that moment. A nice touch that twitching business and the camera jumping! But such an attitude does not take into account the character of the man, and having questioned him closely about it I am satisfied that he did not sit down and cold-bloodedly contrive a story that nobody would be able to prove *did not* happen. What Arthur Shuttlewood saw from his landing window only he knows with any certainty, but it does appear that he saw *something* and that he would have photographed it if he could.

In fact there have been other reports of cigar-shaped objects seen over Warminster at other times. Early one morning in April 1966, four local council workmen saw a huge silvery cigar which seemed to split amidships allowing six small glowing blobs to fall from it and spin away into the distance and there was an almost identical sighting reported a few days later by a Bank of England official motoring in the vicinity.

The odd happenings in Warminster and the villages around seem to have begun on Christmas Day, 1964 when mysterious shock waves descended from the sky on a housewife walking to Christ Church for Holy Communion. The woman, so I am told, was buffeted and frightened and totally unable to explain what had happened. Later other people said they had had similar experiences – and worse.

Consider this one, which Arthur Shuttlewood records in his book *The Warminster Mystery*,* concerning a Mrs Kathleen Penton who claimed to have seen something like a 'flying railway carriage with the windows lit up.'

This is what the author says she told him: 'It was fantastic – so much so that my husband and daughter thought I was definitely going round the bend when I told them about it later. I was opening an upstairs window (about 8.35 p.m.) as it was a stuffy night, when I saw this shining thing going along sideways in the sky from right to left. It glided over quite slowly in front of the downs. Porthole type windows ran along the whole length of it. To my eyes, it was the size of the whole of a bedroom wall – enormous. These windows were lit up, the colour of yellow flames in a coal fire.

'It was very much like a train carriage, only with rounded ends to it. And it did not travel lengthways, but was gently gliding sideways.'

Yet another report came from Mrs Patricia Phillips, wife of the Rev P. Graham Phillips (at that time Vicar of Heytesbury) who said she had watched a brilliant cigar shaped object glowing in the sky for more than twenty minutes. It was just after 9 p.m. in June 1965. The object had first been seen by her twelve-year-old son Nigel who happened to glance out of the vicarage study window while doing his homework. He called his parents and his brother and sister, and the whole family watched the dazzling apparition, taking it in turns to view it through a small telescope.

The telescope was little more than a toy but it enabled them to confirm that the object, which hung vertically in the sky, was indeed cigar-shaped and appeared solid. The lower end was thicker, and seemed to have a ring round it. After a while it

* Neville Spearman Ltd

seemed to grow shorter, as if the object were turning on its axis, and soon after this it disappeared.

'It seemed to be metallic and was reflecting sunlight, but I did not see any exhaust flames or anything like that,' Mrs Phillips told me. 'I am not suggesting it was a flying saucer. I just don't know what it was and I am not prepared to go any further than that.'

A few nights later the same object, or one like it, was seen again and rumour had it that a man who had viewed the object through a powerful telescope had been warned by the police to 'keep his mouth shut' about it. But when I put this to the police, a spokesman said: 'The funny thing is that nobody at all got in touch with us about the object. The first we heard of it was through the local newspaper.'

The police did, however, have an explanation for the noises, or some of them, that people said they had heard at night. The noises were probably caused by flocks of geese going over, they thought. Geese did make weird noises sometimes.

By September 1965 the Warminster Thing, as everyone called it, had been seen by more than two hundred people and thousands of visitors flocked into the town in the hope that they too could catch a glimpse of it.

Since then there have been many more sighting reports from the area and enough information has been jotted down by Arthur Shuttlewood to form the basis of a second book. He is good humouredly aware that many attempts have been made to hoax him as the arch-saucerer of Warminster over the past few years, but stoutly maintains that a large proportion of the sightings and hearings he has reported will stand up to any amount of critical investigation.

At one time the number of saucer reports seemed to be getting so completely out of hand that it was decided to hold a public meeting in the town and try to clear up the mystery. Predictably it was a failure. The meeting was crowded, but a number of people who might have helped to put the matter in true perspective stayed away, presumably for fear of being involved in embarrassing publicity.

Whatever the reason it certainly seems that Warminster since Christmas 1964 has been under concentrated 'attack' by UFOs, explain them how you will. But why Warminster? Is there anything in its geographical situation to make it, for example, an easy target for UFOs? Is there anything 'they' want from the district that is not so easily come by elsewhere? Is it possible that other towns in Britain, indeed in the world as a whole, have just as many odd visitations but are not as acutely aware of them? And what about the chronicler of the Warminster sightings himself? Could it be that without his presence in the town we should have heard little or nothing of the UFO 'attacks'?

I am sure that a less sensitive, less diligent reporter would have made a lot less of the circumstances, dismissing many of the reports without taking the trouble to look into them. Certainly his conviction of the extra-terrestrial nature of the UFOs must play an important part in the way the stories are put over to the public, but this is not to suggest the slightest conscious attempt to elaborate.

Shuttlewood himself theorizes somewhat romantically that Warminster is pin-pointed not so much because of its geographical position but because in the long past some homing device was established in the area making it easy for saucer crews to get their bearings, perhaps to make secret landings for water supplies which, if they are in any sense human, they would certainly need. His own view is that UFOs are always lurking in the Wiltshire skies and can be seen by anybody who has the patience to look for them.

A vantage point for observation is Cradle Hill, to the west of Warminster railway station. Hundreds if not thousands of visitors have climbed this hill for sky watch week-ends. It was to Cradle Hill, indeed, that I made my way with Shuttlewood that drizzly day in May. In fact I made two visits. In the afternoon I went by myself, saw nothing and heard only the critical comments of an invisible bird calling 'Cuckoo!' I got soaking wet. But in the evening when Shuttlewood joined me the rain had ceased although the sky was dismally overcast.

It was a little past 11 p.m. and we stood up there in the darkness with the wind picking at our raincoats, waiting impatiently for something to happen. Once or twice the sky cleared enough for a lonely star to peep through here and there, but there was no mistaking the fact that they *were* stars. Once a jet aircraft zoomed by above the clouds but there were no sounds that could by any stretch of imagination be called mysterious; no strange whirrings, hummings or whistlings;

only the soft soughing of the wind. Towards midnight even Shuttlewood, whom I gathered habitually spent hours on this hilltop, was beginning to be restive. As for myself, I was thinking the whole idea of UFOs was ridiculous and wondering how soon I could reasonably suggest leaving Cradle Hill and heading for my hotel. I began edging towards the road back, then stopped and pointed towards the dark horizon where an amber light had abruptly appeared and was apparently pulsing in the sky – too high up to have anything to do with road traffic.

It was much too big and bright to be a star and there was no indication that it had anything to do with aircraft. There was not a sound of an engine and the light just hung there, not moving a fraction from its position. After a few minutes it vanished but reappeared again later in exactly the same place. Then it vanished again and when it reappeared a second time it was accompanied by another almost identical light behaving in an identical fashion. Car headlights perhaps . . . a car parked on a distant hill? Not a chance of it. They were too bright and much too far apart. Presently they went out together and then the original light reappeared for the last time.

Shuttlewood and I watched the performance for at least twenty minutes, hearing nothing but the wind, and then took the track downhill to the road and the town.

It was a strange and, for me, totally unexpected experience, and I know now how easily one can be caught up in the flying saucer mystery. While watching the light (or lights) I had an uncanny feeling that something remarkable was about to happen and an equally strong sense of disappointment when it did not.

I would not dream, on the simple basis of seeing lights in the sky, of drawing any conclusions at all. There could be any number of quite ordinary explanations for them but, in fact, I have not yet been able to think of even one.

6

UFOs at Stoke-on-Trent

It is safe to predict that many more UFO sightings will be reported in Britain and elsewhere in the coming months and years. In view of this it seems strange that there is so little official scientific interest in the phenomena.

The vast majority of sightings in the British Isles are investigated by amateurs, many of whom have formed groups and linked themselves into a countrywide network to simplify and speed up the work of interviewing witnesses and publicizing the more dramatic events. From these groups there appear, from time to time, reports based on inquiries made with such enthusiasm and attention to detail that they could hardly be bettered by Scotland Yard.

One such report, a masterpiece of its kind, was produced in February 1968 by two amateur astronomers (Roger Stanway and Anthony Pace) of Stoke-on-Trent, Staffordshire, concerning a 'wave' of UFOs which troubled (if that is the right word) the county during the months of August, September, October and November, 1967. The report, it was said, was based on information collected from more than two hundred eye-witnesses who had either been interviewed or had submitted written accounts of what they had seen, in some cases both.

Most witnesses were interviewed within a day or so of their sightings; in some cases within hours. What they saw could therefore be assumed to be fresh in their minds and not dulled by the passage of time or elaborated by afterthoughts. The witnesses represented a cross-section of the community ranging from schoolchildren to housewives and professional men, not a few of whom were trained observers in civil or military service.

According to what Stanway and Pace were able to discover there was a great to-do on the Bentilee Estate, Stoke-on-Trent, on the night of Saturday, 2 September 1967. That was the night a flying saucer was seen to 'land' in a field and later take off again. Two women and several children were among the witnesses.

The excitement began just after 9 p.m. The children were playing outside a house in Beverley Drive opposite Wendline Close when one of them, David McCue, saw a brightly glowing object above the roof-tops travelling on a course roughly parallel to the Close. He shouted to the others: 'There's a flying saucer!'

Just then one of the women, a Mrs Stevenson, came out of her house and called to her neighbour, Mrs Bowen, 'Look at that thing in the sky.' She said afterwards: 'It was a scarlet glow and dome-shaped, and was going over the Close towards the fields . . . It was like a wind when it came over but there was no sound.'

All witnesses agreed about the general shape of the object: a disc that was a dull orange colour surmounted by a dome glowing bright red. They thought it 'landed' in a field beyond the end of Wendline Close and Mrs Stevenson said that when it came down the whole field 'looked as though it was on fire – like a bonfire'.

Six children ran towards the place where the UFO was thought to have landed and the two women followed with a dog, anxious for their safety but curious to see what the object was. However they were prevented from getting near because of marshy ground. By this time also the women were becoming increasingly alarmed and decided to turn back and telephone the police. When they returned the object was no longer glowing in the distance but the children told them it had performed a hedge-hopping manoeuvre from one field to another before 'going out'.

David McCue and a friend, Kenneth Harrington, later told investigators that after the object landed the bright red dome 'went out like a light' and the whole thing seemed more of a yellow colour. It remained illuminated for about two minutes and then the yellow also faded out.

The boys ran to the place where they thought the object had come down but the fields were dark and they could see nothing. This was the situation when the police, a sergeant, and two constables arrived in a van, having responded promptly to the telephone call. Another boy, who seemed scared, tried to show the police where the UFO had come down but the search for it was fruitless and the police gave up, laughing and joking about the whole business.

But this was not the end of the affair. As the police left the fields to return to their van, a man shouted from an upper window that he could see a bright light arising from the fields. Everyone turned to look back. The light, now yellow, or orange-white, like a street lamp, appeared to rise about three hundred feet, hold still for an instant and then dwindle out of sight in much the same way as a TV picture vanishes from the screen.

When UFO investigators questioned the police they agreed that they had seen a light in the sky but said it had gone out almost as soon as they turned to look at it. They were inclined to think it was caused by a car headlamp, it was the same colour. A search of the area by daylight revealed neither marks on the ground nor any other evidence that a tangible object had touched down in the fields.

But when Stanway and Pace returned to the Bentilee Estate more than six months later, curious to discover how much eye-witnesses still remembered of the sighting, they found it was still fresh in their minds. Mrs Stevenson told them that when she first noticed the UFO coming high over the rooftops it was 'going round and round like a spinning top'. It had been a mild evening with a clear sky and she had not needed a coat to go up to the fields.

Asked to describe the object in more detail, she said: 'It was like a disc with something on top like a dome and about the size of an aircraft. I saw something like a silver gleam. I could see this as it came down. I wasn't sure that it was a light, more like a silver gleam on it, a grey colour . . . Mrs Bowen and I ran up the fields. We thought it must have landed, and yet we didn't hear anything . . . It came straight down as if it knew where it was going to land. I can't tell if it hit the ground, that I don't know.'

Question: 'What colour was it as it was coming down?'

'Grey.'

'You couldn't see any red at all?'

'Only the big red glow. The fields were lit up with it, and the leaves. You know it was just as if someone had got a great big bonfire.'

Question: 'Could you see where the red light came from?'

'Yes, the round top part – the revolving part, to me. That was red, but the body was grey.'

'What did you feel like? I suppose you were a bit worried?'

'Terrible. I think I was white. The dog's hair stood on end from her tail, all along her back. This happens when she is frightened.'

Mrs Stevenson said that she and Mrs Bowen had only managed to get to the edge of the field where it was thought the UFO had come down because they were unable to cross a brook. The police had turned up within five minutes of their call. By then they were very worried because some of the boys were missing, but after a while the boys came out of the field and reported that they had not been able to find anything.

Question: 'What did the object look like when it took off?'

'There seemed as if there was a green light on it this time, but it was white, it came up white and seemed to be "generating". The light was getting red, vivid red, but it started off orange, as though the power was building up.'

Question: 'Could you hear any sound as it rose up?'

'No sound – nothing.'

'When it came up, how did it rise? Did it go from side to side or did it shoot straight up?'

'No, it moved up slowly, the same speed as when it "landed". Slow, as if it were cushioned on air – an air cushion underneath it, as though it were never on the ground.'

In reply to further questions Mrs Stevenson said that when she first caught sight of the object above the rooftops she thought it was an aircraft in trouble and about to crash, but when it got closer it looked nothing like an aircraft and seemed as if it knew exactly where it was going. After it had come down and lit up the fields the red glow was not suddenly extinguished but seemed to fade out slowly.

In summarizing the Bentilee sighting, Stanway and Pace made the following points which indicate the objective nature of their approach to the subject of UFOs in general:

1. There is strong corroborating evidence that one, or perhaps two, similar unidentified flying objects were observed shortly after 9.00 p.m. on Saturday night, 2 September 1967;

2. The appearance of this object or objects was completely alien to the observers;

3. The motion of the object which appeared to 'land' was unlike the normal action and operation of a conventional aircraft;

4. The descriptions of the object, or objects, made by different witnesses agree in basic configuration and detail within the limits of human error and memory;

5. The descriptions of the unusual 'landing' motion of the object and its subsequent 'take off' all agree in principle;

6. The presence of the object, or objects, in the vicinity of habitation caused fear and anxiety to a number of the inhabitants.

7. It was the unanimous conclusion of all who had witnessed the strange objects, that these were completely unknown in their experience and could not be explained.

A total of seventy sightings within a radius of about twenty miles of Stoke-on-Trent were outlined by Stanway and Pace. Some, they admit, must have been genuine misidentifications of aircraft or natural phenomena seen under unusual circumstances. Errors of human judgment and memory had also to be taken into account, especially since many witnesses were children who might have let their imaginations run away with them. But, as they pointed out, the fact that people make mistakes should not be regarded as justification for dismissing the whole mystery as 'bunk' and flatly denying that UFOs exist at all.

Not the least encouraging aspect of the investigation, incidentally, was the negative attitude of many witnesses, their unwillingness to report seeing unusual objects or even talk about them for fear of ridicule. It was only after careful persuasion that some of the more detailed and inexplicable sightings were brought to their noticc, the investigators say.

One of these concerned a Mr J. D. Stotter of Doxey, Stafford, who was confronted with a UFO while driving a lorry along the M6 Motorway of the evening of Tuesday, 17 October 1967. Mr Stotter was driving south and approaching the turn off to Holmes Chapel. The sky was clear, with some scattered cloud. It was still fairly light although some vehicles already had lights switched on. Suddenly he began to have an eerie feeling he was not alone, that somebody or something was nearby.

Almost immediately, he said, he noticed through the top

left-hand corner of the windscreen a strange craft moving in the same direction along the left-hand side of the motorway. The object was fairly low in the sky, comparable in size to a Boeing stratocruiser on its first circuit of an airport before coming in to land. He had seen many large aircraft coming in to land at Manchester's Ringway Airport.

Mr Stotter, driving at between thirty-five and forty miles an hour, was able to keep pace with the UFO which he later described as being 'like a large applepie dish' with no real colour to the main structure: it was just a dark mass. He had the impression that there was no paint on the hull and even thought to himself that it could do with a coat of paint.

The understructure was rounded with a group of circular lights or portholes towards the front. He could not remember how many portholes there were but said the colour was consistent with ordinary white light. Above the rounded section he saw what appeared to be a rim and from the rear of the rim came three continuous mauve-blue flames which he thought were the vehicle's exhausts and which streamed backwards and downwards.

Above the rim was a taller structure narrowing off to a flat top which seemed to be illuminated in the same way as the 'portholes'. Mr Stotter had plenty of time to observe the strange craft. After keeping it in sight for a distance of five and a half miles (which he checked the following day) he pulled into the stopping lane of the M6 and watched for a further ten minutes. The craft was travelling quite slowly, he said, and he could hear a sound like a jet aircraft only of a higher pitch, rather like air rushing from the pinched neck of a balloon.

'Suddenly,' he said, 'the craft veered to the left and came almost to a standstill, turned and accelerated back the way it had come but at an angle to the road, disappearing in a few seconds.' As it crossed in front of him he could see the mauve-blue jet streams again; they seemed to straighten up behind the vehicle as it shot away.

Mr Stotter told investigators that he had not reported the sighting to the police because he thought he would be laughed at. Although they were other vehicles on the road at the time nobody else appeared to have noticed the craft. He was quite sure it was not a conventional aircraft. He had been in the

RAF for a number of years and had received training in aircraft recognition.

The Brogans and the Turners, two married couples who live opposite each other in Brieryhurst Road, Kidsgrove, Stoke-on-Trent, were saying good night when Mr Turner noticed what he thought was a shooting star. The time was about 11.10 p.m. on the night of 4 August 1967. All four people stood staring up at the shooting star. But it did not behave like a shooting star for it came right down out of the sky, changing direction on the way. It also slowed down as it dropped from the sky and came to a 'standstill' above the roof-tops at the end of the road. It also grew bigger and they could see it had the shape of a disc which seemed to be metallic with a bright red dome on top. The disc hovering in front of the watchers seemed between eighty and ninety feet across spanning a distance equivalent to two bungalows placed end to end. And underneath the disc they could see a ring of fifteen to twenty rotating red lights.

After hovering for a few seconds the object began to move and disappeared at a fantastic speed over buildings to the west. Neither when it approached nor when it disappeared again did the thing make the slightest noise.

This was the story that the four people told UFO investigators in the course of interviews after the sighting. The way the object appeared, moving at great speed, its abrupt change of course, the way it hovered and then shot off again could not, they said, be paralleled by any ordinary aircraft. Both couples said they were quite shaken by the incident and firmly believed they had seen what they termed as a flying saucer.

In their report Stanway and Pace are emphatic that the story was told them in good faith, and that there was no attempt at leg-pulling. 'We came to the conclusion,' they reported, 'that they had genuinely seen a flying object at close quarters which appeared unusual in shape and motion, and which they could not identify with any kind of conventional aircraft.'

Not the least curious thing was that in the course of the interview Mrs Brogan said this was not the first UFO she had seen. In fact she had seen one almost identical in appearance over more or less the same spot seven years earlier. She and some other children had watched it hovering for several minutes while they ate sausage rolls. It had not made any noise and presently it had moved slowly away and disappeared behind some houses. Her husband had often teased her about this 'space ship' she claimed to have seen.

Yet another strange sighting reported by the astronomers occurred about 8.30 a.m. along the Middlewich Road. Two newspaper boys, David Jones and Peter Hollander, were cycling along the road towards Crewe after finishing their morning round. They were approaching the bridge across Valley Stream. The weather was dull and dry with a light breeze and a lot of cloud.

Suddenly, David, who was ahead, spotted an object approaching them in the sky about a mile away to the left and called to his friend to have a look. At first the boys thought it was an ordinary aircraft but when it came nearer they realized, they said, that it was a 'flying saucer'. It must have slowed down abruptly for in a few moments it was hanging almost motionless in the sky directly above them.

In his excitement, not looking where he was going, David rode into the kerb and Peter collided with his back mudguard. A car coming up behind them sounded its horn as they both fell off and scrambled from their machines. By this time they were anxious only to get under cover.

'We were scared,' said David, 'and we dived under a hedge and looked up.'

From a crouched position they could see the understructure of the object and stared at it for about thirty seconds before the thing made off so rapidly that they could not keep track of it.

A short account of this remarkable daylight sighting appeared in the *Daily Mail* of 31 August 1967 under the heading 'Flying Saucer Hovered over Newsboys', and drew the investigators' attention to them. The boys, aged thirteen and twelve respectively, were interviewed a few days later. They described the UFO as being oval in shape and silver in colour with a transparent dome through which they had been able to see dark clouds; they had also seen what appeared to be a cross projecting at one side. As the object came towards them Peter had noticed a small yellow light at the front, and later, David had seen what he thought were exhaust openings at the back.

The boys said the 'undercarriage' of the craft appeared about the size of a half-crown piece held at arm's length. David estimated the height of the things as about one hundred feet. They could see the underneath quite clearly and said this had a silvery perimeter with an inner oval which appeared to be largely comprised of millions of black tubes or wires against a silver background. Along the centre ran a silver rectangular section containing three identical solid black circles, one towards each end and one at the centre (sketch 3).

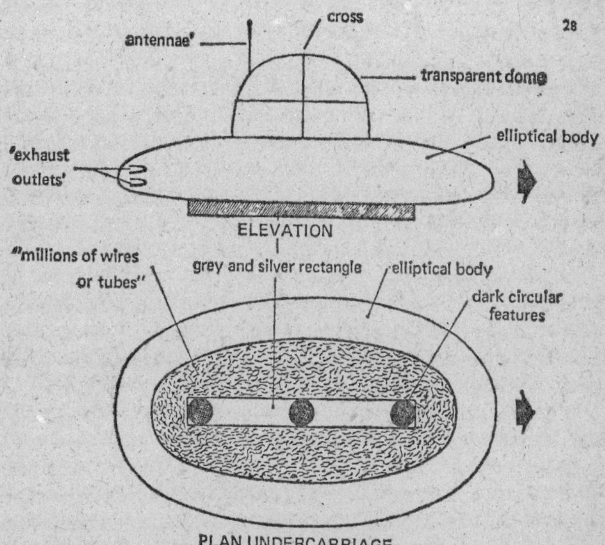

3. The UFO of Stoke-on-Trent

Commenting on their interview with the boys, Stanway and Pace remark: 'The whole episode seemed incredible but after an hour of questions and answers and the boys' calm attitude to the extraordinary experience, we came away feeling that this was a genuine account and that they had in fact observed at close quarters the operation of an aerial craft of unknown origin.

'It could be asked why the passing car carried on apparently unaware of the UFO. On reflection, however, it is very unlikely that the occupants of the car could possibly see an object which was near yet almost above them in the sky through the restricted view of the car windows.

'From the newsboys' story the apparently deliberate motion of the strange craft could have indicated that it was directed by intelligent control, particularly when it hovered above them as if observing their actions and perhaps also their reactions to its presence. Could it be that this aerial vehicle, completely unfamiliar in appearance, was in fact a remotely controlled surveillance craft which had detected the boys as they moved along the road and had come down for a closer look?'

The first thing to be noted about the foregoing sightings is that in all cases the observers saw much the same sort of object. There was the wide understructure and there was the dome on top which at night glowed a bright red. In all cases, too, the object seems to have had some interest in the observers, as if observing them in return. The manoeuvres carried out were pretty similar also: the swooping out of the sky, the hovering, the rapid disappearance. And the silence.

It should not be forgotten, however, that inasmuch as all this is evidence at all, it is only hearsay evidence. Ufology as a science, if it can be so called, is at a big disadvantage in that investigators cannot deal with first-hand evidence; there is none. They are obliged to consider not the substance but the 'shadow' of things which other people claim to have glimpsed and to form judgment based on the characters and qualifications of the observers whose memory may be faulty or whose motives suspect. In addition there are complicated psychological factors to be considered.

We may begin by asking ourselves: were the people listed in the four sightings all liars? Is it conceivable that in Mr Stotter, in the women and children at Bentilee, in the neighbouring couples at Kidsgrove and in the two newsboys, that Stanway and Pace picked on a group of people without the slightest regard for the truth? It seems very unlikely. In any case why should they want to tell untruths? Possibly they were jointly involved in a carefully worked out plan to hoax the investigators? This again is patently absurd, apart from the fact that there is no evidence that any of the separate groups were even distantly acquainted with the others.

Then what about hallucination? Perhaps, to take the case of

Mr Stotter, one might be tempted to think that he was 'seeing things'. After all, on his own admission nobody else using the M6 appeared to notice the UFO he described. Indeed if nobody else anywhere in the area had seen anything at any time, Mr Stotter's evidence would certainly look pretty odd to say the least. But this, as we have seen, was not the case. Other people in and around Stoke did see quite similar objects at other times. The same argument can be applied to the newsboys, but in the other two cases there were too many witnesses for the hallucination theory to work. Could all these people have suffered the identical hallucination?

What it clearly boils down to is that the women and children of Bentilee, the Brogans and Turners, the newsboys and Mr Stotter must all have seen *something* whatever it may have been. It was certainly not something in their own eyes. It was something in the sky; something that their accounts of it suggest was not moving in any haphazard fashion but with deliberation and purpose – in a way, that is, which could hardly be ascribed to any natural phenomenon like ball lightning, the planet Venus or even an artificial satellite or lump of space debris decaying in the atmosphere.

It is hardly necessary to add that in these four sightings the observers could not have mistaken conventional aircraft for UFOs. To begin with none of the UFOs made any noise and as we know to our cost, ordinary aircraft make a considerable amount of noise. The glowing object that 'landed' in the fields at Bentilee may have behaved to some extent like a helicopter but it quite clearly was not one. Had it been a helicopter this could have been established in a very short time once the police had been called in.

One is left facing the very odd conclusion that all these people really did see a flying machine or machines which, for the time being at any rate, cannot be explained in familiar terms. This is certainly what they themselves believe.

The Staffordshire Report was widely circulated to interested bodies including the Ministry of Defence, Stoke-on-Trent City Police, the Central Electricity Generating Board, the officer commanding RAF Tern Hill and Air Traffic Control at Birmingham and Manchester Airports. In addition, the two astronomers had an interview with officials at the Defence Ministry to discuss the report.

The following letter was later received from the Ministry:

Dear Mr Stanway,

When we met last month I promised to write to you about your Flying Saucers Report.

First I should like to say that those of us in the Department who read the report were very impressed by the amount of time, effort and enthusiasm put into the project by you and Mr Pace. Since we covered the ground fairly extensively at our meeting, I hope you will forgive me I set down our views fairly briefly.

The Ministry of Defence's approach to the question of unidentified flying object reports is quite straightforward. Each report we receive is fed into our air defence system and we are able to call on the highest scientific and technical advice within the Department. We also take advice, where necessary, from other government departments and outside bodies such as the Royal Observatory, the Meteorological Office and the British Museum. Reports are examined in sufficient depth to establish that there are no air defence implications and that they can be reasonably related to known phenomena. But we do not undertake to pursue each report until we have established an indisputable correlation with a known object. So far we have found no evidence of air defence implications or of craft under extra-terrestrial control.

We have an open mind on the possibilities of new evidence and are interested to see the results of serious studies such as yours. Your report has been examined carefully and although we have found much of interest, we are unable to find any new scientific evidence in it.

I am sure you will have found from your own investigations, that prompt reporting is often a prerequisite of positive explanation. The sightings covered by your report were between eight and sixteen months old when we received them. In view of this lapse in time we do not feel that an examination in depth by the Department at this stage would be likely to produce positive explanations. We are, of course, ready to look at any new reports from your area, but I must emphasize again the virtues of promptitude in these matters.

Finally, may I thank you personally and on behalf of Mr

Cassie and Mr Dickison for taking the trouble to come and see us.

Yours faithfully,
L. W. Akhurst

After studying the letter, Stanway and Pace wrote back as follows:

Dear Mr Akhurst,

Thank you for your letter of 23rd July and for the kind sentiments which you expressed.

Although the contents of your letter were not unexpected, Anthony Pace and myself were nevertheless disappointed that your letter did not tell us anything that we did not know already. We are surprised that you have made no reference to the fact that certain events described in our Report appear to be without explanation in terms of natural or man-made phenomena, especially as Mr Cassie, Mr Dickison and yourself were unable to offer any explanation for the events that took place on Saturday, 2nd September, 1967. We can understand Mr Cassie's reaction when he said that he thought it was rather worrying that no explanation could be found for the 2nd September sightings, but we fail to see why you should then say that the Ministry is unable to find any new scientific evidence in our Report.

Also, we submit that the presence of unidentified flying objects in the vicinity of Stoke-on-Trent on 2nd September, 1967 and directly under the Amber 1 air route has definite air defence implications and at least warrants a full scale investigation to discover why it is not possible to identify these 'unknown aircraft'. We appreciate that at the time of the sightings it would have been difficult to locate and identify these objects by means of our air defence system, as for most of the time the objects appeared to be no higher than a few hundred feet from the ground, and therefore, well under our radar detection network in this country.

We are sure that the Ministry is aware of the danger inherent in the false assumption that unknown flying machines cannot possibly exist if they are not detected by this country's radar network and defence system.

We also consider that steps should be taken to find the

owners and pilots of these 'unidentified aircraft' as it does appear that prosecutions should be brought for apparent breaches of a considerable number of air laws and flying regulations. However, the fact that there were no identification markings or signs on most of the flying objects described in our Report does present problems.

Normally the lapse of time between reports and the investigation into them does materially effect the possibility of finding explanations. However, in our case, we must again confirm that our Report only contains the salient details of sightings, and on our files we have the very fullest accounts and detailed drawings made by witnesses within days and sometimes hours of their sightings.

Therefore, we must stress that investigations were made as soon as possible, and naturally, we should be very pleased to give you any further information that you may require. We must again confirm that a personal visit was made to a member of your department on 29th September, 1967, when the events of the previous month were fully described to him.

We were told that even if the Ministry wanted to interview witnesses and make its own field investigations, it could not possibly do so, as the Ministry did not have the necessary money, facilities, equipment or personnel to carry out such investigations.

We are very worried about this inability to make the necessary investigations, and that is one of the reasons why we visited you on 20th June this year. We hoped to persuade the Ministry to change its policy by releasing all information relating to unexplained reports to the scientific world in general so that some serious research could be done at universities and scientific colleges.

Naturally, we are dismayed that the Ministry's policy is one of treating all reports as confidential and that there appears to be a complete reluctance to investigate and solve scientific mysteries of this nature.

However, we hope that we may be able to interest various scientific bodies in the subject, and if you have any further information or advice that may assist us in our investigations we should be very pleased to hear from you.

Yours faithfully,
A. R. Pace and R. H. Stanway

7
Essex Revisited

There is a tantalizing Will-o'-the-Wisp quality about UFOs. Although sightings tend to occur in waves (which some ufologists suggest coincide with the nearer approaches of Mars) nobody can tell precisely when or where the next individual appearance will be. And because the duration of any sighting is apt to be short the chances of taking snapshots occur only rarely.

Even people on sightseeing holidays with cameras round their necks often fail to make use of them when abruptly confronted with a UFO in the sky. Either they are too astonished to think of using the camera or there is insufficient time to focus once they have thought of it. Not infrequently, in the cussed nature of things, the last negative has been used up anyway.

All this, though disappointing to investigators listening yet again to a story of lost opportunity, is nevertheless quite natural and argues in favour of a claimant's good faith.

But once in a while everything clicks, including somebody's shutter; and this was so in the case of two intelligent young women motoring in Ireland on Boxing Day 1965. Miss Jacqueline Wingfield, a granddaughter of the great Lord Jellicoe, and her Danish friend Miss Mortensen were driving near Cappoquin on a perfect day with a clear blue sky. The time was between 3.15 and 3.30 p.m. Suddenly Miss Mortensen caught sight of a strange object moving steadily across the sky in front of them.

She barely had time to point towards it before Miss Wingfield braked the car to a standstill and switched off the engine. Both women reached for their cameras. Miss Mortensen in the passenger seat was the quicker and having got out of the car just had time to take one shot of the UFO before it disappeared.

Later Miss Wingfield told me: 'It was a round solid looking object flying from right to left across the horizon and there was a trailing plume like flames behind it but no smoke and the thing made no sound. I don't know what it was but it was certainly not any kind of ordinary aircraft. The thing itself looked bright and metally.'

When she returned to London, Miss Wingfield reported the sighting to her colleague Mr Charles Gibbs-Smith, the aviation historian who took charge of the negative and arranged for it to be developed by a specialist photographer.

'This is the most extraordinary flying saucer phenomenon,' he told me. 'We've got its pedigree from first to last, with no loophole for faking.'

The photograph showed a bright object about the size of a pea with a pale plume billowing out behind it. The object had been too far off for detail to show up but, as Mr Gibbs-Smith pointed out, several important conclusions could be drawn from it. The thing was clearly not a cloud. It was not a conventional aircraft of any sort. It was not a balloon, a rocket or a sputnik. Nor was it a meteorite.

In a letter he wrote to *The Times* Mr Gibbs-Smith unequivocally referred to the object as a flying saucer and suggested that it might be powered by an anti-gravity motor. Such a motor, he said, would account for the fantastically high speed and manoeuvrability of UFOs in general. It was well known that many laboratories on earth were engaged on gravity research although it was one of the hardest things to get anyone to talk about it, so high was the security.

In support of his belief that the object was a flying saucer from another world, Mr Gibbs-Smith said the reason people in general were so set against the interplanetary notion was that we were such an ineradicably conceited civilization.

'All the astronomers agree now,' he wrote, 'that the stuff of the universe is more or less the same and that there may be thousands – or millions – of inhabited planets in space. We can only boast 6,000 or 7,000 years of civilization. What of a civilization that can boast 70,000 or 700,000 years. Their minds may be completely different from ours. They could probably do almost anything: de-materialize: ride light beams; keep themselves in cold storage for hundreds of years. We're kittens in civilization. People *will* forget that the first aeroplane flew in 1903; and here we are, sixty years afterwards, already orbiting the earth.'

A schoolboy, of Leslie Avenue, Conisborough near Doncaster, also showed great presence of mind when he snapped a flight of 'saucers' in March 1966. Stephen Pratt, then aged fifteen, was returning home with his mother from a fish-and-chip shop when they noticed a single bright light in the twilight sky to the north-east. They watched the light for a few minutes before arriving outside their house.

It was orange-coloured, rather deeper than the nearby sodium lamps in the street but of the same brightness, and it seemed to be pulsing as it moved slowly towards the west. Stephen went indoors to tell his father and brother and at the same time to get his camera. When he came out again the light was still there and he just had time to focus the camera and take one shot.

The strange thing was, however, that when the film was developed at a local chemist's, instead of the light in the sky Stephen found he had a picture of three aerial objects flying in line astern, the second and third appearing smaller as if in perspective. All three were similar in shape, closely resembling conventional 'saucers'. Just how the objects could have been photographed when they were not visible to the observers is hard to explain. Cameras do, of course, play tricks. Light gets in and spoils an otherwise excellent picture, or curious blemishes turn up on the negative. But in this case it was a remarkable coincidence that an attempt to photograph a strange light in the sky (which might have been a UFO) should yield 'blemishes' that looked like flying saucers.

Dr Geoffrey Doel, chairman of the British Unidentified Flying Objects Research Association, who is a member of the Royal College of Surgeons and an expert radiologist, is sure that the photograph is genuine in that it was not deliberately faked. He reported after examining it: 'It is most unlikely that a young boy using a cheap camera could have made a fake negative like this.'

The same would appear to be true of a remarkably similar box camera picture taken four years earlier by fourteen-year-old Alexander Birch of Moor Crescent, Mosborough near Chesterfield. Alex was in the back garden of his home taking snapshots of his dog along with two school friends when they noticed something unusual in the sky. Alex aimed his camera and clicked the shutter. When the film was developed he found he had a picture of a group of objects apparently flying in formation – objects astonishingly like those later snapped by Stephen Pratt.

Again one has to accept that the picture *could* have been a photographic freak caused by some camera defect; but again it appears that the picture resulted from a deliberate attempt to photograph something in the sky. A teacher at Westfield Comprehensive School who questioned Alex and his friends seems to have been satisfied that they did not fake the picture, for he was later quoted as saying: 'What they saw is anybody's guess. The boys said the objects made no sound. They just hovered.'

Except in the case of Warminster, which seems to have rather more than its fair share of sightings, it is rare for a UFO to be seen over precisely the same locality more than once. The thing causes a stir at Brighton, say, and that, for the time being, is that. The next appearance might be over Bangor or Bootle or even Bratislava. Nobody can predict with any certainty when and where the next sighting will be.

But if a UFO is seen hovering over a certain area of Essex between 30 June and 2 July 1971, it will be rather more than a coincidence. This date has been suggested by Mr Alan Watts, a meteorogolist and author of some excellent books on weather forecasting, whose work has convinced him of the extra-terrestrial nature of UFOs.

The suggestion was made in a report to *Flying Saucer Review* which Mr Watts wrote following a sighting over Halstead, Essex on the morning of Friday, 1 July 1966. This sighting as he pointed out, took place five years almost to the day after a similar sighting at Halstead. This made it 'almost unique' and drew from the author the comment: 'If I'm still in this locality between 30 June and 2 July 1971, I shall be disappointed not to see another unidentified flying object glinting in the mid-summer sun . . .'

His argument was that although UFO sightings always seemed a random phenomenon, perhaps here was evidence that they in fact occurred much more regularly than was thought. The randomness might be largely due to the fact that people, especially those living in towns, were much more inclined to look down than up, and therefore probably missed a good many opportunities for observing UFOs.

The first he knew of the sighting on 1 July 1966, Mr Watts said, was when he was telephoned about 8.20 a.m. by the College keeper of the Technical College at Colchester where he lectured in physics, and was asked if he had seen the shining object over Hilly Fields, an open space to the west of the College building. The object had been in view for a full hour and lots of people had seen it.

'It did not take long to locate the object high in the western sky,' Mr Watts said. 'It was bright and silver and shone. There seemed to be at one time an orange glow on the top part. It looked as though it were slowly revolving. By naked eye it looked at times like two objects one above the other but closely coupled. The upper one gave the impression of roundness while the lower part seemed fuzzy.

'My thoughts turned to one of the cosmic ray research balloons that are sometimes flown from Cardington (Beds) by Bristol University and Imperial College. It had that sort of look and the fact that I thought so and then changed my mind is significant.

'Anyway, having been caught before, I got a parallel rule and began to make chinagraph marks on my west-facing upper window pane and to write times under them. From these I was able to confirm a very slow drift of the object to the right, i.e. with north going components. At about 8.45 a.m. it disappeared. The College observers lost it at the same time or nearly so.'

Mr Watts said that from calculations made by himself and at the College it had been possible to estimate that the object was between 40,000 and 45,000 feet up. He added that when he came to plot the object's position on a map he realized how near its position was to that of the first object seen over Halstead at 9.30 p.m. on 30 June 1961 – five years and eleven hours earlier.

Could it have been a balloon? There was an easy way to check. Mr Watts obtained details of high altitude wind speeds which might have influenced the object's behaviour. From this information it appeared that had the object been a balloon it would have drifted between thirty and forty miles during the hour and half it was under observation. Yet to all intents and purposes the thing had remained stationary. When eventually it did move it moved *against* the prevailing winds.

'This convinces me,' Mr Watts said, 'that the object could not have been a balloon however much it may have looked like one.'

Several witnesses helped in assessing the size of the object by holding a ruler at arm's length and checking its apparent dimensions. All made a calculation of between two and three millimetres which when scaled up to a distance of about fifteen miles gave a diameter of between two hundred and four hundred feet. Compared to this a cosmic ray balloon of a million cubic feet capacity might inflate to a diameter of one hundred feet, but only when operating at an altitude above 50,000 feet. Apart from this it was learned that no balloon had been launched from Cardington at that time.

Then there was the observation of two of the night staff of the Technical College who said that while they watched, a star-like object, much smaller than the stationary one, left the latter and shot off at high speed in a south-easterly direction. They were quite certain of this.

'So what was this thing?' Mr Watts asked. 'Whatever it was maintained its position in space for a long time except for a certain drifting about against winds which would certainly have swept a balloon much nearer the observers if not actually past them.

'My own hunch is that this was another of the vast carrier craft which drop into our atmosphere from time to time to despatch scout saucers on unknown missions, one of which *was* observed. The fact that it so resembled a sky-hook balloon may be chance or design and makes reassessment of other presumed balloon observations worth consideration. In any case it was a vast object and was observed also from the Wattisham RAF base.'

In the original Halstead sighting on the night of 30 June – 1 July 1961 there had been a good deal more aerial activity and Mr Watts gathered more than two dozen eye-witness reports. Pairs of lights apparently hanging in the sky at a height of 40,000 feet were seen over a wide area but not so far from Halstead as to outrule the notion that they have come from a central source. One pair of observers reported seeing a ring of between six and nine lights. Several others said they caught a glimpse of a dark metallic object in the sky.

Mr Watts collected the eye-witness reports following a letter he had published in a local Essex newspaper, and wrote in a report based on the letters that a strange cigar-shaped craft about 250 feet long appeared to have taken up a position two to three miles north-west of Halstead. It had occupied this position, keeping more or less stationary, from at least 9.30 to 9.40 p.m.

'During the hovering period,' he said, 'it exhibited two lights of extreme brilliance. By my own observations at nineteen miles distance their apparent brightness was two-to-four times as bright as Jupiter which was particularly bright at that time.

'The estimated height was of the order of 13,000 feet. At the end of the period of hovering the craft turned north, suddenly made a noise akin to a turbo-prop and flew away in a climbing arc towards the north. One witness describes it as having portholes which in fact fits the same type of object depicted in *Flying Saucers Have Landed* (Plate 11).

'The background sky was light with cirrus cloud still illuminated by the sun and thus these portholes must have been self-luminous patches to have been visible against the sky.

'The general impression was of a blue-grey body when seen without the aid of binoculars. One witness was emphatic that the object had a wing, which seems feasible. The lights faded as the object accelerated away. None of the witnesses saw it again.

'There were, subsequent to this, pairs of lights seen over a wide area but so far away as to preclude the contention that the large cigar-shaped object was the parent craft which released smaller craft.

'These were observed in the interval 2130-2210 as a pair somewhere over the area of Grays . . . A further pair were observed at 2140 travelling east probably over Dedham and also at great height . . .

'Between 2210 and 2225 a ring of 6-9 (precise number unknown) lights "roosted" in the approximate area the carrier had occupied and again were probably at around 40,000 feet or higher. The impression one gets is of a fan-out from this centre in the period following 2130 to perform some set of tasks unknown and return to rendezvous in the same spot.

'Some "saucers" were about until at least 0320 next morning. Two hovering lights "the size of tea plates" were observed at this time from Kelvedon in the direction of Mersea Island . . .

'Useful speculations are that "saucers" have limited range probably due to physiology rather than mechanics and the appearance of a crop of saucers demands a carrier craft to have launched them and presumably to re-embark them.

'The lights were described as red or orange during accelerated motion and yellow-white during hovering. Thus one is led to think that the light is somehow essential to the hovering process. It is significant that red-orange-yellow-white stem from photons of increasing energy or put another way from bodies of increasing temperature. The light is an outward manifestation of energy being evolved in the physical act of hovering.'

Another UFO sighting which Mr Watts investigated in his own neighbourhood was reported by Mr Paul Green of West Mersea, Essex, whom he later described as 'as straight a witness as you could hope for'. Mr Green, who is employed by a heavy engineering firm, was certainly not looking for publicity and his story would not have come out had not his mother reported it to a local newspaper.

The date was Sunday, 19 September 1965. Mr Green was riding his motor-cycle from Colchester to Mersea Island at about 1.30 a.m. when he heard a strange humming noise which seemed to come from all round him. At first it was low pitched 'like a child's humming top', but rose to a high pitched whistle, then abruptly died away.

Looking to the east he saw a blue pulsating light coming in very fast at an elevation of between twenty and thirty degrees. At the same time his motor-cycle engine failed, so he pulled up and raised the machine on to its stand. Looking up again he saw a large saucer-shaped craft descending on the marshes about a mile away. Mr Green estimated that the diameter of the saucer was roughly equivalent to the top of a gas holder – he works in the shadow of a gas works. He said that there appeared to be a ring of spheres around the under side of the craft 'like a ball race'.

The object had a dome which was a kind of translucent blue and pulsated in the manner of a heart beating. The whole structure was self-luminous and well defined against the sky.

When the object sank on to the marsh it disappeared behind hedges but the pulsating light was still visible. Mr Green tried to start his motor-cycle again and when it would not start he began to push it along the road. After another try, it did start and he got astride it and continued his journey, looking back over his shoulder until he could no longer see the glowing object. Questioned about the incident later he said he felt a tingling sensation as the saucer was coming in to land and felt numb from the effect. He said he did not investigate the saucer because he felt scared.

Was there anyone else on the road? Yes, Paul had seen a man on a scooter, but even after the story had been published the man did not come forward to say that he also had seen the saucer.

Was there any corroborative evidence? Apparently one of Paul's workmates saw a blue light race across the sky over Colchester at about 1.15 a.m., or fifteen minutes before Paul's sighting.

'And then there is a rather amazing coincidence,' said Watts. 'The week-end following the one in question we had some of my wife's relations from Ruislip, Middlesex visiting us. Before we had a chance to recount any details of this incident they told us how they had been awakened at 2 a.m. that same Sunday morning by a noise which was just like a humming top but much louder. Those were their very words.

'The times of 1.15 a.m. over Colchester, 1.30 a.m. at Fingrinhoe and 2 a.m. over Ruislip are all commensurate with the same device.

'There are a few observations which are worth making. The noise is interesting and as Paul was in the direction of deceleration its change of pitch might be some form of Doppler effect. The numbing sensation may only occur along the line of deceleration and is probably of the same physical cause as that which stopped the engines of the two bikes.

'I personally visited the area of the landing on the Saturday after the sighting and ranged it with field-glasses. There was, however, little to be seen.'

It is important to remember in connection with the Halstead sightings that Mr Watts is a professional scientist trained in aircraft recognition and making meteorological observations. He is thus more accustomed than most people to looking at the sky and less likely to misinterpret what he sees. As a physicist he is also accustomed to objective thinking and weighing scientific evidence. When I asked him to sum up his views on UFOs he replied unhesitatingly: 'There is no shadow of doubt in my mind that these objects are extra-terrestrial'. Nor was this a snap judgment but one arrived at after some years of interest in the subject.

Fundamentally, Mr Watts believes there are at least two major kinds of UFOs: the large cigar-shaped vehicles and smaller disc types varying in size. The evidence, he says, is that the cigar-shaped craft are transporters bringing the saucers (some of which are remotely controlled probes) into the atmosphere and releasing them for an assortment of research tasks. It is through their behaviour and our own knowledge of physics that we should eventually be able to understand what they are doing in our skies.

From his own inquiries, Mr Watts says, it appears that despite official 'knocking' of the subject people generally have accepted the notion that flying saucers do exist and would not be unduly disturbed if UFOs became 'respectable' and were given proper research attention by orthodox science.

Basically, it appears that UFOs operate in an 'upper octave' area of the physical spectrum which is unfamiliar to us but which may not require an especially difficult break-through to understand. Superior technical knowledge, for example, apparently enables operators of extra-terrestrial craft to become 'invisible' by deflecting radar beams in such a way that they fail to register the presence of an object. One theory is that they do this by emanation of a strong electro-magnetic force field. They may also be able to make themselves invisible in the optical sense by bending light rays in much the same way as a lens does, or to camouflage themselves as objects which are familiar to us. Camouflage is, after all, an art which has been practised on this earth for many centuries.

What kind of experiment could scientists carry out to determine the existence of UFOs by studying their behaviour? One example Mr Watts gives is this. Motorists have often reported that under the influence of a UFO their car engines have stopped. Could electro-magnetism cause this effect? To find out Mr Watts experimented with his own car. He put a coil round the ignition system and generated a strong alternating magnetic field while the engine was ticking over.

The experiment was not an unqualified success because the

field was not strong enough but the result was good enough to demonstrate that people who have claimed that their engines died on them were not necessarily suffering from delusions. In Mr Watts' case there was a distinct power failure as soon as the generator was switched on. He is careful to point out, however, that the experiment does not necessarily prove that the physical effects radiated by saucers – which for instance interfered with the running of Paul Green's motor-cycle – are primarily electro-magnetic. It could be, he says, that electro-magnetism, gravitation and the physiological and mechanical effects described are the end result of a deeper physical continuum whose nature we have yet to comprehend.

8

Strange Marks on the Ground

If UFOs are indeed manned spacecraft from other worlds one rather mortifying fact has to be faced: their crews are evidently not too keen to make our acquaintance. At any rate nobody can say they go out of their way to do so. Presumably it would be no more of a problem for a flying saucer to land, say, in Hyde Park than in the Californian desert. But, alas, they do not do it; or they have not done it yet.

One begins to wonder indeed whether we shall ever have a real get-together. A few people here and there may be able to claim acquaintance with the Venusians, Martians or whatever, but how about the rest of us? And the question may now be asked: Is there any *real* evidence that UFOs have ever landed anywhere?

If a strange aircraft from another part of the world managed to get through Britain's air defences, touch down in a field and take off again, it would surely leave behind some evidence of its visit even if the craft itself were not seen by anybody or only seen from a distance?

At the very least, it would seem, there would be marks on the ground to show where the aircraft had landed and taken off again – especially if the emergency landing site happened to be under cultivation.

It has to be admitted that in places where UFOs have been *seen* to come down nobody searching the ground afterwards has ever found any indisputable clue to a landing – not in the British Isles at any rate. But there have been some curious happenings and disturbances to the ground which some investigators have attributed to UFOs. Not long after the big autumn flap of 1967 a Sunday newspaper headlined a story: 'UFO RIDDLE OF DAMAGE TO FARMER'S CROPS'. The story began:

'What caused the damage in two farmers' barley fields in the Isle of Wight? For weeks agricultural experts and aeronautical scientists investigated the strange whirligig patterns left in crops flattened along a narrow strip three-quarters of a mile long.

'Now the scientists, led by Mr Leonard Cramp, an aeronautical technician with the British Hovercraft Corporation claim: "It was, without doubt, the path of an unidentified flying object as it was coming in for a touchdown".'

The farmers who owned the damaged fields, it was said, were not impressed by this notion. They did not believe in flying saucers. On the other hand they could not supply any alternative explanation. They had neither seen nor heard anything to account for the damage. There were no people, animals or farm gear which could have flattened the barley in the vicinity at that time and there had not been any storms or even a little wind and rain.

Mr Cramp speaking for a team of UFO investigators said: 'We checked everything else it could have been and drew a complete blank'.

But it was not entirely from a process of elimination that a flying saucer was blamed for the crop damage, for in the course of their inquiries the investigators found out that just before the damage was discovered an unidentified flying object had been seen by two boys attending Whippingham Primary School near Newport, Isle of Wight.

The date was 10 July 1967. The boys were lining up to go into school. It was a quarter to nine on a fine, cloudless morning. Suddenly one of the boys nudged his friend and pointed high up at the northern sky. In the distance a milky-white disc was hovering. They could not look at it for long because they were already moving forward to enter the school building but when they came out for a break at 10.30 a.m. they peered up at the sky again.

At first they could see nothing except the sky itself. Then – there it was again, or a similar object, away to the west. Other boys were now watching with them. Altogether a dozen saw the strange object which they estimated to be 'larger than a bus' moving westward. A moment later they saw it begin to fall, fluttering down like a leaf as though out of control; then, when it was almost on the horizon, it seemed to correct itself and began to climb again but was almost immediately lost to sight behind some trees.

There was nothing more. The object was not seen again on that day or any day following, but on his way home on the evening of the sighting one of the boys looking out from the top of a bus saw the strange marks in a barley field bounded by the Newport-East Cowes road. And in the report he subsequently wrote on the whole affair, Mr Cramp said: 'Investigations of this site revealed large areas (up to six yards wide) of damage, in the form of depressed and flattened stalks, which made an almost completely circular pattern. The damage had a very mechanical appearance in a vortex pattern, sometimes clockwise and sometimes anti-clockwise, but predominantly clockwise. The centres of some of the vortices had tufts with broken stalks and others had nothing – obviously the roots and stalks had disappeared completely.

'In these areas the heads of corn had been denuded and looked (to quote one farmer) "as if they had been thrashed".'

At first it was assumed that the damage was restricted to the area near the school, but aerial photographs showed that it was much more extensive, continuing through three fields and roughly parallel to the roadside hedge. Towards the end of the run the damage was appreciably less, suggesting that at that point whatever had caused it was not longer in as close contact as it had been to begin with.

What seemed particularly significant to the investigators was that the length of the run appeared to correspond with the distance the boys thought the object had moved westwards from the time it had fluttered down to the time it regained control and started up again.

'When the extent of the damage to their fields had been seen by the local farmers,' wrote Mr Cramp, 'they could not accept the idea that the weather, which had been very fine preceding the discovery of the damage, could have caused such effects. They agreed, individually, that the damage was too localized to be the result of any natural causes known to them, and one farmer said: "It looks as though a mad thing has gone through there".'

The possibility that the damage might have been caused by straying cattle was quickly ruled out by comparison with a nearby field in which cattle were known to have strayed. There was not the slightest similarity between the two effects.

The sight of dogs gambolling through the barley, which

sprang up again immediately after they had passed, just as quickly disposed of the notion that smaller animals, even had there been herds of them, could have been responsible.

There remained the possibility that freak winds might have caused the damage but a professional meteorologist who was consulted about this said it was out of the question, especially in view of the fact that not only did the damaged area run parallel to the hedge but made some precise right-angled turns and even neatly skirted a dilapidated hut. Apart from this the barley had been attacked with such violence that a wind causing it would have been an extremely noisy wind.

In the course of searching the area for clues the UFO investigators found a number of stones, some quite large, strewn along the trough made in the barley fields. They also collected a total of a hundred and thirty feathers from a wood pigeon, suggesting that the bird had come to a violent end. But there was nothing which pointed to any ordinary explanation for the damage. Nothing indeed fitted the facts more readily than the notion that an aircraft of some kind had come down in difficulties, skidded along by the hedges, recovered and taken off again. Had it been a helicopter or any other familiar aircraft this surely would very soon have been discovered.

The strange assault on the Isle of Wight barley fields was not the first event of its kind to mystify people in Britain. Four years earlier, in July 1963, something very odd happened in a potato field at Charlton near Shaftesbury, Wiltshire, which got a lot of publicity when the police and an Army bomb disposal squad were called in.

One morning a farmer, Mr Roy Blanchard, arrived to work in the potato field and found among his crops a crater eight feet in diameter. There was nothing to show what had caused the crater. It looked as though it had been scooped out by an enormous spoon. Mr Blanchard seems to have been in no doubt that the crater was formed by a spaceship that landed in the field.

'I didn't actually see it,' he told reporters, 'but what else could it have been? Obviously some craft from outer space since it sucked out my barley and potatoes when it took off.'

This may not be the first explanation that would have occurred to anybody coming across a hole in a field but Mr Blanchard was sufficiently convinced, it appears, to put it forward to the Bomb Disposal Squad at Horsham, Sussex. No doubt they took it with a pinch of salt but they came and spent quite a few hours digging in the crater in search of metal which had been detected by their instruments.

The investigation of the Charlton crater was then unexpectedly complicated by the arrival of a gentleman described as an Australian astro-physicist who claimed to have discovered two other marks in adjoining fields. It was clear to him, he said, that a flying saucer had landed in difficulties, bounced along and taken off again from Mr Blanchard's field. The marks were similar to marks found in Australia in 1954 and 1955 and in France in 1958. He himself had seen the marks in Australia and believed they were caused by a space craft.

According to a *Daily Telegraph* account of the Charlton mystery the Australian was a Dr Randall who had been called in by the Army to give expert advice. He had expressed the opinion that the saucer was five hundred feet wide, weighed six hundred tons and had a fifty-man crew.

It was Dr Randall also who drew attention to 'burned' grass and ash-covered leaves in a corner of a hedge abounding the potato field. This, apparently, was where the spacecraft had crashed through the hedge on taking off. The *Telegraph* quoted him as saying: '. . . we think these craft are coming from somewhere in the region of Uranus. Each one would take several years to make the return trip. They would be due about now after the last one in France.

'We think their mission is peaceful and exploratory. They may well be worried or curious about our atomic explosions for their stability may depend on ours. They are not more than a hundred years ahead of us scientifically. The type of spacecraft of which we have evidence is a kind which we can comprehend and will quite likely be making ourselves inside a century.'

This was splendid stuff. But, alas, further investigation ruled out the notion that the hedge and grass had been 'burned'. The blackening it appeared was actually due to nothing more sinister than mildew. The Army then issued a statement calling for 'a note of sanity' in the whole business, and surprisingly declared that Dr Randall was unknown to them. His assistance had not been sought and he had no official standing.

Because metal had been detected by their instruments the Army team went on digging. The crater may have been caused by a bomb – that was their main interest in the excavation – and if so some evidence of this might be found. Otherwise the only 'reasonable' suggestion was that a meteorite had caused it – a suggestion favoured by most orthodox scientists at the time. And when eventually a 'fused-looking' half pound lump of rocky substance was dug up the matter seemed settled.

Not everyone was satisfied, however, and on 29 July 1963, Major Patrick Wall, Conservative MP for Haltemprice, asked the Secretary of State for War what had been the findings of the Army team and whether there was any evidence to justify the notion that the Charlton crater was made from an extra-terrestrial source.

Mr Godber: 'The Army Bomb Disposal team which excavated the crater at Charlton have found no conclusive evidence regarding its cause. The small object which was initially thought to be a meteorite appears in fact to have been a piece of local rock and was not the cause of the crater.'

Major Wall then asked what were the findings of 'two Royal Air Force officials' who investigated the crater and whether investigations were continuing.

The reply: 'From my inquiries I have no reason to think that anything happened in the area which could justify further investigation by the Air Ministry.'

On 1 August Major Wall tried again. He asked whether the crater was still of interest to the Army. Mr Godber replied: 'The Army was concerned to discover whether the crater could contain an unexploded bomb. Nothing of this nature was found and the Bomb Disposal unit left the site on 26 July.'

From the foregoing it is evident that the authorities were only too anxious to wash their hands of the Charlton affair; but what is interesting to other people, particularly those with a bias in favour of flying saucers, is the admission in the Commons that 'no conclusive evidence' was found to account for the crater. This admission was considered 'highly satisfactory' by the late Waveney Girvan, founder and former editor of *Flying Saucer Review*, and easily the most persistent investigator and critic of Whitehall policy on UFOs of his time. The crater, he wrote, in a detailed report, was a complete mystery – and that was official.

It was Girvan who published the first full description of the crater. It was no simple hole in the ground apparently. 'The marks comprised a saucer-shaped depression or crater eight feet in diameter and about four inches in depth. In the centre of this depression there was found a three feet deep hole variously described as from five inches to one foot in diameter. Radiating from the centre hole were four slot marks, four feet long and one foot wide.'

Mr Girvan, who also interviewed Farmer Roy Blanchard, 'a man of sound common sense', attributed to him these words: 'There isn't a trace of the potatoes and barley which were growing where the crater is now. No stalks, no leaves, no roots. The thing was heavy enough to crush rocks and stones to powder. Yet it came down gently. We heard no crash and whatever power it uses produces no heat or noise. I believe that we have received a visit from a spaceship from another world.'

In this connection, Girvan drew attention to the fact that a local policeman, PC Anthony Penny, had reported seeing an orange object flash through the sky on 10 July and vanish near the field in which the strange marks were found. As regards the half-pound 'meteorite' (which he had never believed to be a meteorite in the first place) Girvan reported that it had in fact been found to be a piece of common or garden iron stone which could be found buried all over Southern England. It had been identified as such by Dr F. G. Claringbull, Keeper of the Department of Mineralogy at the British Museum.

'The importance of the piece of iron stone now becomes apparent,' he wrote. 'If ordinary iron stone is widely distributed and highly magnetic, the Bomb Disposal Unit's detector would not be of much value. If violent reactions were obtained from the Charlton object then it must have been magnetized in some way, perhaps, by the proximity to a force field. This proves, in the first place, that the whole affair was not a hoax. Some evidence would surely have been apparent on the surface of the field, but nobody can suggest that the iron stone had been planted: the British Museum suggested that it had been buried in the ground for some time . . .

'I would say that in all probability a machine of unknown origin landed in Farmer Blanchard's field some time in July and then took off again. The behaviour of the Army goes a long way to support this theory. The sense of the matter rests with Farmer Blanchard who, when faced with conventional explanations replied: 'But where have my crops gone ?" '

Girvan was highly critical of the part played by 'Dr Randall' whom he seemed to think had been deliberately introduced to bedevil the Charlton inquiries. His idea was that if you produced somebody whose authority seemed beyond question and who was later strongly suspected of talking nonsense, then the whole investigation could be put to ridicule and the true facts of the case conveniently obscured. The reason, he pointed out, that the Uranus theory was given so much publicity was because Randall seemed to have been 'adopted' by the Bomb Disposal Unit. Sergeant James Reith had declared that he had met Randall at Woomera and had said of him: 'You can take his name as an authority on flying saucers'. But Southern Command at Salisbury had later explained this curious endorsement as being due to the excitement of the moment.

'It is interesting to ask,' Girvan commented, 'if excitement on what the Army describes as a routine job leads to a misinterpretation of this magnitude, what would happen if the men of the Bomb Disposal Squad got really worked up ?'

In his search for the truth of the Charlton story Girvan looked around for (and found) other instances of holes and craters appearing mysteriously in the British Isles. There were in fact several which had been discovered either just before or just after the Charlton crater. Of these probably the most significant was at Flamborough Head. A young man cutting hay on his father's farm had come across a ten feet wide shallow hole which had not been there when the land had been top dressed in the spring. The hole had been reported to the police but neither they nor anybody else could suggest anything to account for it satisfactorily. The hole had jagged edges and was surrounded by cracks. In addition earth had been scattered around it.

On the slopes of Dufton Fell, Westmorland farmers Bill Richardson and John Rudd had discovered two craters, one of them about sixty yards across and about two feet deep. There was evidence in this case that soil had been washed away along a narrow gully but some local people had recalled that similar craters had appeared on the fell tops, mystifying their parents, more than half a century ago.

At this time also a park area in Bristol had been roped off for Bomb Disposal men to investigate a hole in the grass discovered by employees using a mower. It was believed that a meteorite was responsible. And on 27 July the BBC Scottish News reported: 'Three more mystery craters. A bomb disposal squad have been having a look at them in a field near Sanqhar, in Dumfriesshire. No trace of metal or explosives has been found. The craters are similar to those found on a hillside in East Lothian; scientists were having a look at them today.'

To town dwellers accustomed to walking on concrete, asphalt and granite, the notion of holes suddenly appearing in the ground may seem more than a little odd, even though subsidences do occur in towns from time to time. Water, possibly from a leaking supply or drainpipe, loosens the subsoil and the surface gives way. But out in the open country the surface is often anything but firm and easily weakened and washed away by heavy rainfall. Therefore, one should not, I suggest, be unduly surprised at the discovery of a hole in a field, even a pretty big hole.

Out in the open also, a meteorite falling from the sky could leave its mark without anyone seeing it happen. Animals too may rough up the ground without leaving any special clue to incriminate themselves. As a young reporter I once investigated the case of a mysterious circle, twenty-five feet across, that someone came across on Chislehurst Common. The circle, bounded by a shallow ditch, was at first thought to have some archaeological significance. In fact, it had been made many years earlier by horses' hooves. For it had been the practice, I discovered from an eighty-year-old villager, for grooms to take horses belonging to the local gentry out to this part of the Common for exercise. The grooms would stand in the middle of the clearing holding the reins while the animals in response to a whip galloped round in a circle.

However, it does not appear, either in the case of the damaged barley fields on the Isle of Wight or in that of the Charlton crater, that any ordinary explanation will do. Neither animals, the weather, nor meteorites seem to have been in any way responsible. At the moment both cases remain unsolved and the choice is to forget about them (as most people will do) or keep them on file (as a few will do) in the hope that further evidence will turn up.

Not the least bizarre feature, common to both incidents, is the way crops disappeared as though rooted out and carried away by a mechanical excavator. But however the crops were removed, one can be pretty sure that it was not due to the ground giving way under them; otherwise some evidence of this would have been discovered, especially in the case of the Charlton crater. So the possibility that the damage may have been done by flying saucers which came down with engine trouble and then took off again when all was well is probably no less fanciful than any other solution one might care to put forward.

9
Inquiries at Scoriton

The Father of the UFO cult, if it be no more than a cult, was undoubtedly the late George Adamski, co-author of the book *Flying Saucers Have Landed*, published in 1953. Adamski was the first man to claim that he had made contact with someone from another world.

The story is pretty well known, but since some of the details form a necessary background to this chapter I beg leave to recall them if only briefly. Adamski, born of Polish parents who emigrated to the United States in the 1890s, was an amateur astronomer who lived on the slopes of Mount Palomar where the world's biggest telescope is situated and from the vicinity of which he did a fair amount of star-gazing himself with a six-inch private instrument.

On 20 November 1952 Adamski and a party of friends were enjoying a picnic lunch when, as the story goes, a large cigar-shaped object, plainly a spaceship, appeared over the mountain ridge. To Adamski its appearance meant one thing: that whoever was in the ship wished to make his acquaintance, so he asked two of his companions to drive him along the highway to a point where he could set up his telescope and camera which intuitively he had brought along for such an encounter. When the apparatus was ready he sent his two companions away, asking them to rejoin the rest of the party and watch carefully from a distance.

A few minutes later, Adamski afterwards claimed, he noticed a flash in the sky and almost immediately a small scout ship evidently despatched from the bigger aeroform came gliding down from between two mountain peaks and settled out of sight behind a hillock a mile away. Adamski had managed in the meantime to take snapshots of it. Then, after pocketing the negatives, he became aware of a man standing about a quarter of a mile away at the entrance to a ravine. Moving towards the man Adamski saw that he was wearing what appeared to be a ski suit and had long sandy hair reaching to his shoulders. The newcomer seemed to be a pleasant sort of chap and Adamski quickly felt at ease with him, even after it flashed through his mind that he was in the presence of a being from another world. Not surprisingly perhaps the visitor did not speak English, but despite this formidable disadvantage he was remarkably skilful at making himself understood. In fact he and Adamski chatted together for a good hour largely by means of signs and telepathy. Adamski was able to learn, for example, that the spaceman came from the planet Venus and that his attitude, indeed the attitude of all Venusians, towards earthmen was absolutely friendly although some concern was felt for our scientific progress, especially in atomic energy.

The spaceman escorted Adamski to the hillock behind which the saucer in which he had arrived was hidden and nothing untoward happened except when Adamski inadvertently stepped too close to the metal rim of the machine and got a slight electric shock. Despite his evident desire to be friendly, however, the spaceman declined the earthman's request for a ride in the saucer. Presently, stepping lightly back into the thing he soundlessly buzzed off.

Adamski's friends, who had obediently kept watch, admitted afterwards that they had seen him talking to someone in a brownish garment. They also claimed to have seen two sets of footprints, one of which was obviously their friend's and the other, a smaller set, which seemed not to go beyond the area in which he said the saucer had landed.

A sequel to the contact claim came a few weeks later, in December, when according to Adamski the saucer returned and hovered within a hundred feet of where he was standing in Palomar Gardens. A hand was thrust out from one of the port holes and a film negative holder (which the spaceman had 'borrowed' on the first visit) was dropped. It was on this occasion that Adamski managed to obtain some of the close-up saucer pictures, the veracity of which has been argued about ever since; but when the returned negative was later developed it was found not to contain a picture of the saucer in flight but what appeared to be a message in hieroglyphics which nobody has yet succeeded in deciphering – if indeed it were a message.

The sensational nature of *Flying Saucers Have Landed* ensured that it would be a best-seller. Adamski became at once a hero and a villian, a madman and a saint. You took your choice according to what you wished to believe, because it soon became evident that nobody was going to prove one way or another whether the author was hallucinated, deliberately lying or telling the simple truth. By and large the supporting evidence of his companions did not amount to much. Although they testified to seeing the cigar-shaped object, the man in the distance and the footprints, somehow they did not seem convinced that it all added up to the arrival of a visitor from Venus. Well, they were a long way off, weren't they?

When George Adamski came to London in 1964 I telephoned him at the small hotel where he was staying and was courteously granted an interview in the time he had to spare before leaving to give a lecture. I do not remember having any serious personal interest in the man, but I suppose I regarded him as a likely subject for a newspaper story. It would be something to say I had talked to him and if I could trick him into an admission that the Venusian encounter was nothing more than a hoax I could depend on getting sizable headlines out of it.

I did not know enough about him to have formed any clear impression of the sort of man I was going to meet but, if anything, I expected an individual of obvious wealth (he must have made a packet!) and of rather hectoring, go-to-blazes manner. One would have to be, surely, to have withstood all the publicity, criticism and abuse that had been hurled at George Adamski. In the event I found a modest, soft-spoken man with a gentle, patient face, who answered every question fully and politely, without the slightest attempt at evasion or the slightest show of hostility, and who was evidently prepared to go on answering as long as I cared to put the questions. Nor, as far I could see, was this due to his having become accustomed to cross-examination although he must have had more of it than almost any man alive.

I could not now quote any of the questions I put to him, but they were all aimed at getting him to repeat to me personally what he had written in his account of the Palomar experience in the hope that some embarrassing discrepancy would reveal itself. Adamski, a lean, weather-beaten man with thick, iron-grey hair, responded easily and without hesitation in support of his remarkable claim. It had happened and that was that. If anyone believed him he was glad; if they did not it was too bad but what could he do about it? Long before I left him I knew I was beaten as far as tripping him into any incautious admission was concerned. Adamski was so damnably normal and this, I think, was the overall impression of him that I carried away. He *believed* he had made contact with a man from Venus and he did not really see why anyone should disbelieve *him.*

I told myself that if he were deluded he was the most lucid and intelligent deluded man I had ever met. When, some years later, I came to write his obituary, I found it a melancholy task.

Since UFO phenomena are reported in great numbers from all over the world, it is obviously impossible for even the most painstaking investigator to question everyone who claims to have seen a flying saucer. In practice I have found this applies even to a small country such as Britain where many more sightings are reported than is generally realized. Even the task of tracking down and interviewing witnesses of the more remarkable events of this sort is quite prodigous. One has to rely heavily on reports in newspapers and periodicals devoted to ufology.

One man I should have spared no effort to cross-examine had I known of his existence in time was Ernest Arthur Bryant, who worked as a groundsman at an old peoples' home in Newton Abbot, Devon. But unfortunately no sooner had I heard of this man and the remarkable events said to have befallen him that I heard he had died.

Bryant's claim was no more fantastic in essence than Adamski's, but there were factors that made it even harder to swallow. Indeed, to anyone considering the case on face value, without any knowledge of the man himself, it must have seemed a load of fraudulent rubbish involving, it appeared, the suggestion that Adamski had returned from the dead and that 'proof' existed that Captain Mantell's aircraft had in actual fact tangled fatally with a UFO.

Fortunately, however, the case has been documented by pretty conscientious investigators who were themselves quite evidently sceptical at the outset. The conclusions they reached are set out in an admirably thorough report by Eileen Buckle.*

* *The Scoriton Mystery* (Neville Spearman)

Miss Buckle, who interviewed Bryant on several occasions, described him as an ordinary family man living with his wife and three children in the village of Scoriton. An ex-seaman and war-time commando, Bryant had worked as a security officer in Gibraltar, and later trained as a prison officer. At the time of the investigation he was fifty-one, with a deeply lined, out-of-doors type of face, a warm friendly manner and a good sense of humour. Miss Buckle noticed, in fact, a fair resemblance to Adamski himself.

What Bryant claimed was that on 24 April 1965 (incidentally the day after Adamski died) a large saucer-like object appeared to him over a field near his home, hovering about three feet from the ground, and that a door in the saucer opened to reveal three figures, dressed in what appeared to be diving suits and helmets, who spoke to him and even allowed him to inspect their vehicle.

Bryant admitted he was pretty much taken aback although he managed to resist the temptation to run away. After watching him for a few moments, he said, one of the three beckoned him with both arms outstretched, whereupon he lost his original fear and began to climb over the iron gate in a fence separating the field from the lane along which he had been taking an evening stroll.

In a statement made later Bryant said: 'As I approached, they began taking each other's helmets off and I stared at them in astonishment. Two of them had extremely high foreheads which came to a point. Their features were thin and sallow and there was no facial hair. Eyebrows and eyelashes were fair and fine and their hair, which was longer than ours, was between a blond and a mousy colour. The nose was squat and the eyes very blue in colour with a vertical cat-like pupil. Then I realized that they each had only four fingers to each hand, tapering, of equal length, and more widely spread out than ours. There were no thumbs.

'When I first saw them their breathing was laboured, but after some minutes this seemed to wear off. The third person had a normal appearance – there was nothing to distinguish him from you or I. He had short brown hair, very dark brown eyes and appeared to be a youth of between fourteen and fifteen years of age.

'The three wore suits of a silvery colour which made a

sound like tinfoil as they moved. The young one's suit struck me at the time as being a size too large, and the belt hung loose. The boots were similar to ours in design, having two straps, one at the toe and one at the ankle; the soles were very thick, I should guess about one and a half inches. When they moved no sound whatever came from the boots.'

It was the youth, Bryant said, who appeared to be the leader of the trio. He introduced himself as 'Yamski', speaking English with the suggestion of an American twang, although the name had given Bryant the impression that he might be Russian. If it was not 'Yamski', it was something like it. When asked where the trio had come from he replied: 'We are from Venus'. Then, apparently responding to the blank look on Bryant's face, he had turned to the others and added: 'If only Des (or Les) were here, he would understand'.

It was this part of the conversation that intrigued the UFO investigators at the same time as it sounded a jarring note of warning that Bryant, knowingly or otherwise, could be party to an elaborate hoax. The name 'Yamski' was all too much like 'Adamski' for the coincidence to go unremarked, and the Des-Les bit seemed an absolute cinch to refer to Desmond Leslie, co-author of *Flying Saucers Have Landed.*

But questions phrased to discover whether Bryant had read the book or knew anything at all about Adamski or Leslie drew a blank. No books on the subject of UFOs were found at his cottage, and he insisted that before the alleged contact with the Venusians his interest in flying saucers had been minimal. In fact the investigators formed the impression that Bryant was completely unaware that there was anything sensational in this part of his conversation with the saucermen; indeed it had seemed rather meaningless.

As a mechanically-minded man he was agog to have a look inside the spacecraft and try to discover how it was propelled. His interest, he said, was evidently appreciated by the crew who assisted him to step up into it and took him on a short conducted tour of the interior which, he discovered, was divided into three roughly triangular compartments. There was no furniture other than a sort of couch in each section and a kind of TV screen with coloured lights moving rhythmically from bottom to top. Subdued lighting came from a triangular 'globe' at the high point of the ceiling. The only garment to be seen in the craft was draped across one of the couches: a purple robe, rather like a dressing-gown, with a rose embroidered on one sleeve.

Because he could neither see engine control gear nor feel the vibration of a running motor, Bryant had asked Yamski how the machine could possibly fly. Yamski had replied firmly: 'Ideo-motor movement', which meant nothing to his questioner.

Then the spaceman added something else which was incomprehensible to the countryman. He said: 'Watch for the blue light in the evenings, in a month's time we will bring you proof of Mantell'.

Bryant's last sight of the trio was after he had jumped down from the spacecraft and moved about ten yards away. By then they had put their helmets on again and were standing at the doorway waving goodbye. A moment later the door closed, the saucer rose to a height of ten or twelve feet and abruptly vanished.

But this was not the end of the story; according to Bryant, the Venusians kept their word to return with 'proof of Mantell' in a month's time. It was 7 June at about 10.30 p.m. when Bryant became aware of a low humming noise, gradually increasing in volume. He left the cottage to see what was causing it and immediately noticed 'a blue light' coming from a shadowy UFO approaching overhead from the south-west. As the thing passed over the cottage there was a sound which he described rather oddly as 'like the slamming of a castle door with a long corridor behind'.

The following morning, after getting up at his usual time of 5.30 a.m., he was wheeling his motor cycle from the cottage to the lane when he saw on the ground a piece of metal of curious shape (rather like a bracket with a bolt going through it) which seemed to glow in the half-light. Nearby were several other pieces of metal. Bryant collected them and put them in his haversack. Later he searched the area again and found a glass phial containing silver sand and a piece of parchment with two words written on it in a language he did not understand.

It was only after this event that Bryant decided to say anything about his experiences, and the first person he told was his wife whom, he stated, did not believe him. But it so happened that his two younger children overheard the conversation and repeated the story at school. As a result the story soon got around the village and Bryant found himself answering questions, usually a little less than serious, from neighbours and the local police who had apparently got hold of the idea that a Russian spaceship had landed in Bryant's back garden.

In an effort to put the matter right and save himself further embarrassment, he wrote to a local newspaper, although continuing to refer only to the second sighting. The second sighting, he thought, was bad enough. But who would believe the first? However, the whole story eventually came out when on filling up a form for the British Unidentified Flying Object Research Association (BUFORA) he admitted that the blue light sighting was not the only one.

The glass phial and the pieces of metal were, of course, prime exhibits for the UFO investigators who lost no time in seeking to have them identified by experts, althought his proved a tougher job than they had expected. The parchment itself was not too much of a problem – at least to begin with. The words written on it were in Greek: 'Adelphos Adelpho' meaning 'Brother to Brother'.

Good stuff of course. Possibly intended to show a link between Adamski and Bryant, both of whom, by the way, were of Romany stock and both, apparently, having been singled out for a visit by Venusians. What else could it mean? How else had it got into the field where Bryant found it if it *had not* been dropped by the saucer?

As for the pieces of metal, especially the screwy looking piece, excitement rose when it was identified as part of an aircraft bomb sight; but, alas, it could not be positively identified as coming from any particular one. And as far as could be ascertained nothing was missing from the wreck of Mantell's plane that could not be reasonably accounted for.

The foregoing account of the Scoriton mystery is necessarily short but I have tried to present the salient features in an objective fashion. Bryant's story is to my mind particularly interesting in the context of UFO investigation as showing the thoroughness with which UFO researchers undertake inquiries into the phenomena and the strange, not to say bizarre cross-currents which seem to bedevil so many cases.

In Miss Buckle's account of Scoriton, for example, it appears that a great deal of time was wasted over incomprehensible messages, described as 'insertions' that turned up in the middle of tape recordings, and also over interviews regarding the pieces of metal with an anonymous 'scientist' who, although it did not appear so to begin with, turned out to be not a little crazy.

It is easy enough, indeed, to dismiss the whole of the Scoriton business as nonsense. But that to my mind is neither a satisfactory nor scientific way of dealing with it. One cannot say that *nothing* happened at Scoriton. Whatever the reason for it, something *did* happen. An apparently normal British countryman and family man, respected by his friends and neighbours, came forward to say that he had seen a flying machine from another world and spoken to the occupants. Why should he do this? There seem to be three possibilities. He could have been a liar set on achieving notoriety at whatever cost. He could have been suffering from some monumental delusion. Or he could have been the victim or perpetrator of an elaborate hoax.

It certainly does not appear that he was telling lies. Miss Buckle sums him up thus: 'One could not help feeling that whatever his limitations might be he was essentially a good man. He also gave the impression that he was as sober as anybody you are likely to meet, not the sort of person who might play a silly joke . . .' And one could add to this that Bryant apparently realized the risk he ran of being looked upon by his friends and family as being a bit of a crackpot – the sort of reputation that nobody cares to have.

Was Bryant then suffering from delusions? This seems the stronger possibility, yet much the same objections can be made here as can be made against the notion that he was a liar. None of his friends seem to have had any cause to suspect him of any kind of mental trouble; they found him perfectly normal. Apart from this, the UFO investigators would almost certainly have noticed it if he had displayed any peculiarity. They are accustomed to dealing with 'odd balls' and sooner or later would assuredly have been exchanging significant glances behind his back. There are all too many little ways in which a person with a fixation, however reasonable he may seem on the surface, gives himself away. Not infrequently he is over insistent about his own honesty and nearly always he is repetitive. Bryant, on the other hand, appears simply to have been conversational, ready to answer questions but never to underline his answers with needless emphasis. The fact that he died suddenly of a brain tumour has, in retrospect, to be taken into account. But a lot of people die of brain tumours without having claimed to see flying saucers or any other kind of apparition.

Against the delusion theory must also be put the fact that he did produce 'evidence' of a sort in the form of the metal pieces and the phial – if they were not purely coincidental. Possibly he could have got hold of the metal pieces and submitted them as clues, but the phial with the parchment bearing the words 'Adelphos Adelpho' does not seem at all the sort of idea that would have occurred to a man of his comparatively low standard of education.

To the stubborn rationalist, the third alternative, that the man was the victim of an elaborate hoax, probably makes the greatest appeal. But a moment's reflection must show that the objections to this idea are equally formidable. If the Scoriton affair was a hoax then Bryant must have been a party to it rather than a victim, although, as has already been stated, he was not the sort of person to play tricks of this kind. Otherwise the hoax theory falls flat because of the extraordinary nature of the background needed to set it up. It is inconceivable that any person, or group of people, could have 'staged' the UFO sighting, producing a 'craft' and three 'Venusians' sufficiently authentic to take in a man like Bryant, and then arrange for the whole set-up to 'disappear'. There remains a possibility, of course, that he *might* have had the UFO sighting planted in his mind through hypnotism but there is no evidence that he had ever had any dealings with anyone who could or would even want to hypnotize him.

All that is left, indeed, is the notion that Bryant was telling the truth about something that, however incredible and far-fetched it may seem, actually happened to him.

For the record, I personally find Bryant's story impossible to believe just as I have always found the claims of Adamski impossible to believe. Yet these are not the only contact stories. There have been many others, particularly from America and France. Furthermore, if one accepts the possibility, however remote, that some UFOs could be piloted spacecraft from other worlds, surely it should not be difficult to take a further step and accept that occasionally we are visited by space travellers who want to make contact with us?

What then is the difficulty? Is it simply due to the knowledge that hoaxes *have* been perpetrated and will certainly be perpetrated again? Is it that one can point to at least one case in Britain of a contact claimed with someone from another world which, the evidence suggests, was deliberately faked?

10

Allingham – A Hoax?

An event which made the whole of Britain sit up and take notice occurred in September 1967. It was the simultaneous discovery of no less than six flying saucers positioned in line across the southern counties from Clevedon near Bristol to the Isle of Sheppey. There was nothing indefinite about these sightings. The saucers were really there. Not only could they be clearly seen and photographed, they could also be touched, for they were all on the ground.

The kerfuffle these six saucers caused lasted only a few hours, but in that time squads of police, a bomb disposal unit, an RAF helicopter, and dozens of scientists turned out to investigate them – to say nothing of crowds of ordinary sightseers.

The saucers may have been disappointingly small (they measured about four feet across and were eighteen inches deep in the domed part) but they conformed clearly to the classical saucer shape and from each of them came an eerie bleeping as it lay gleaming whitish-silver in the grass. The first was spotted by two young men out walking near Queensborough, Isle of Sheppey, and the police kept guard over it until a helicopter from Manston whisked it away. Caddie Harry Huxley found the second while hunting for a ball on Sundridge Park golf course, Bromley, Kent. The third was discovered in a potato field at Winkfield satellite tracking station near Ascot, Berks, by engineer Roger Kenyon who discreetly threw pennies at the thing to see if he could get any reaction from the 'little green men' inside. Saucer number four was found by a postwoman at Newbury, Berks, and subsequently examined by scientists from Aldermaston. Number five turned up near Chippenham, Wilts, and was taken to a corporation rubbish dump where a bomb disposal expert blew the top off it – releasing a gush of stinking air. Number six was first spotted by a newsboy on Dial's Hill, ten miles from Bristol.

It turned out, as the country later discovered, that the whole thing was a hoax dreamed up by students from Farnborough Technical College as a rag stunt for charity. The saucers, it appeared, had been positioned overnight near roads and footpaths so that they would be discovered early in the morning. It had cost the students about £30 to build them and put in simple battery-operated bleeping devices to make sure the saucers attracted attention. The smell, described as 'a cross between pigswill and porridge', actually came from a mixture of flour and water with which the things were filled.

It was undoubtedly a good hoax, though possibly a little irritating to officials who were needlessly engaged in investigating the saucers for the better part of a day.

Hoaxes have, in fact, accounted for quite a few UFO sightings over the years and certainly there have been many fakes among the saucer pictures published in newspapers and magazines. The outline of a saucer sketched on a window, for example, can be made to look pretty convincing against the sky beyond. You can hang a model of a UFO by thread from the branches of a tree and achieve much the same effect. Or toss a flat hat, car hub cover, ashtray or similar shaped object into the air and snap it from low down against a tall building. But photographers who study UFO pictures are not often taken in by these devices.

In any case a hoax does not amount to much unless the perpetrator can come forward and say 'I did it'. Normally this is what happens, although there may also be cases in which the perpetrator has felt he went too far and is scared to admit the fake. But it is seldom that a fake picture remains in the records for very long unsuspected.

People who take the trouble to investigate UFO phenomena are usually as keen as anyone else to separate the false from the true, both as regards pictures and reports of sightings. The classical 'lampshade' pictures which George Adamski claimed to have taken near Palomar have long had their critics and could well be audacious fakes, as could his entire story, but if so they have never been denounced as such and a great many people stubbornly believe them to be genuine.

But what of Cedric Allingham who claimed an experience similar to Adamski's and produced comparable photographs following a caravan holiday in Scotland during February

1954? What are we to make of the report he published in book form* more than a year later? Allingham, according to his story, had motored from London and crossed the border on 18 February with nothing in mind other than to study wild bird life. He had intended moving up to Wick and the most northerly part of the Scottish mainland, but events changed his plan considerably. Instead he spent a week in the neighbourhood of Lossiemouth and then motored directly back to London.

Having parked his car and trailer, the story goes, he was taking a stroll along the coast between Lossiemouth and Buckie when he heard the sound of an engine and then a swishing noise overhead. His immediate thought was that a large bird was swooping down on him but the sky above was clear and all he could see, high up, was a dark speck that looked like anything but a bird. Raising the binoculars he habitually carried when out walking, Allingham focused them on the speck and 'realized to my amazement that I was looking at what could only be a Flying Saucer'. The thing glinted in the sunlight, giving the impression that it was made of metal and about the size of a bomber. It was about 5,000 feet up and tilted at an angle which revealed an upper dome and spherical landing gear.

'As I stood staring, my brain temporarily paralyzed, it started to move once more,' the author wrote 'at first slowly then more quickly northwards and upwards. I dropped my binoculars and took three photographs. I knew, as I did so, that this was a forlorn hope. I am only an amateur photographer and a cheap folding camera cannot do marvels. All that I could expect to find on the film were small specks. (Which was in fact exactly what I did find) . . .'

Allingham said he afterwards followed the flight of the saucer with the help of his binoculars again until it disappeared above the clouds which were thicker in the northern part of the sky. Afterwards, reluctant to leave the area, he sat down to have a sandwich lunch and continue to keep a watch on the sky. Then, thinking that the saucer must now be thousands of miles away, he got up and continued walking along the coast from Lossiemouth. Just after 3 p.m. he saw the saucer again and this time, using his binoculars again, he

* *Flying Saucer from Mars*, Frederick Muller Ltd.

was able to make doubly sure that it really was a saucer and not a balloon or any sort of conventional aircraft. By now he was feeling very excited and even went as far as waving at the thing although it was still a good 10,000 feet away. But unfortunately the saucer disappeared again.

Hopeful that it would appear for the third time Allingham resumed his walk, but it was not until he had turned and was walking back to Lossiemouth that he heard the swishing sound again; and there, coming in across the sea was the saucer.

'There was no doubt,' he wrote later, 'of its intention to land. When it was within a few hundred yards of me, I distinctly heard a low humming sound which I imagine could only have come from the engines; this was confirmation of my own theory that Flying Saucers are powered by more or less conventional means – not by mental control or anything of that sort.

'I was too rooted to the spot to do anything for a moment; then I whipped out my camera and took a couple of shots in quick succession, as the saucer was making its final descent. It was heading almost directly towards me. The whole metallic body seemed to glow faintly, and the saucer hovered for a second or two before landing with a soft but audible thud, some fifty yards from where I stood.

'It was indeed a magnificent craft, and its finish would surely be the envy of our aircraft manufacturers. About fifty feet in diameter and perhaps twenty feet high, the hull, central wall and upper dome seemed to be shaped from one sheet of metal. I could detect no joints or bolts. I could not say what the metal was; its colour and lustre were not unlike polished aluminium (although it would of course need to be very much more robust).

'There were two visible groups of portholes set in threes round the central wall, above which was a small flange. From the top of the dome a dark verticle rod projected which reminded me of a lightning conductor. I could not guess its function. The spherical landing gear – at three points just inside the base of the hull – looked as if made of some slightly resilient material similar in texture to rubber.'

As Allingham moved forward, he said, a sliding panel in the lower part of the craft moved back and a man leaped lightly and gracefully to the ground. He added: 'As he advanced to meet me, I raised my arm in salute. He did the same. And then, for a while, we stood staring at each other.

'It is natural that we should have done so. He, presumably, had seen other Earthmen. I had never seen a spaceman. In all essentials, however, our appearance was similar. My own height is five feet nine and a half inches and his was slightly more; I should say he stood about six feet. By terrestrial standards I should say we were about the same age (I am thirty-two), and his hair, like mine was brown and short. But his skin was a curious colour, rather like deep tan. Even so, had he been dressed in terrestrial clothes, I doubt whether he would have had any difficulty in passing for an Englishman. The only difference was that his forehead was higher than that of any man I know.'

The visitor was clad in what appeared to be a one piece suit, covering him completely from neck to feet. Only his head and his hands were bare and he wore no shoes. One thing that Allingham could not help noticing was that the spaceman wore some kind of breathing apparatus consisting of tubes in his nostrils and slender, flexible pipes leading away. But there was nothing frightening in the man's appearance. Allingham's only regret was that he had had no time to prepare a list of questions that he might put to the visitor.

He realized that communication was liable to be a problem anyway; but one thing he must find out was where the saucer had come from. To solve this problem, Allingham said, he reached for a scribbling pad and drew a rough diagram of the sun with three circles round it representing the orbits of Mercury, Venus and Earth.

Showing the diagram to the saucer man he pointed first to the orbit of Earth and then to himself. Next he pointed to the orbit of Venus and indicated his belief that the saucer had come from that planet. To his surprise the stranger shook his head.

Allingham tried again. He drew a fourth circle outside the others and when he pointed to it, at the same time uttering the name 'Mars', the stranger nodded vigorously. This was a real turn up for the book. All along Allingham had been convinced the man came from Venus – just like the men Adamski had seen in the Californian desert. It explained a lot though. It explained why this spaceman did not have long hair and why the saucer which had brought him looked slightly different in shape and had actually landed instead, as in the case of the Venusian saucer, of hovering just above the ground.

'Obviously,' said Allingham, 'it would be impossible for me to discover all I wanted to know simply by making signs and drawing diagrams. Adamski, if I had read his account correctly, conjured up mental pictures and somehow managed to form a sort of telepathic link with his visitor. I wondered if it would be any use my trying to do the same though I had little confidence in myself.

'It was just possible though, that if the Martians had highly developed telepathic powers he would be able to receive my message. I decided to give it a try. Picturing a saucer flying from Mars to the Earth, I asked mentally: "Why have you come here?"

'There was a pause and again we looked at each other. I made another effort at telepathic communication, concentrating hard on my subject, then looked helplessly at him; it was becoming clear that my efforts were not going to be successful! I had a sudden desire to laugh. I pointed to my lips, then to my brain, shook my head and smiled.

'The Martian looked at me and then he, too, laughed. It must have been a ludicrous spectacle – men from different planets standing helplessly on a lonely part of the Scottish coast, laughing at each other's efforts to make one another understand.'

But Allingham, not unreasonably, was anxious at all events to have the visitor know that he wished to be friendly so he relied on the age-old custom of handing over a gift. All he had available was his red fountain pen. Allingham held it out indicating that his companion was to take it. The Martian did, and put it away in an outer pocket of his garment.

There the encounter might have ended for the Martian seemed unaware of any obligation to exchange what he had received for a gift of his own. But, undeterred, Allingham resorted again to his scribbling pad. This time he drew a rough circle (presumably with a pencil) to represent the Red Planet and in the circle he sketched a few lines in the approximate area of the Martian 'canals'. The Martian gave an emphatic nod and uttered some encouraging words in his own language.

What it amounted to, Allingham decided, was that the man was affirming that the 'canals' did exist and had been dug to irrigate the planet. The matter indeed was completely resolved when Allingham pointed first to the sea and then to the 'canal' markings. Yes it was water all right.

'I think,' the author commented later, 'that the truth of the matter is something like this. Millions of years ago when the Martians were of course far less advanced than they are today, the drying up of the water all over their planet was an extremely serious matter for them so they constructed the canals with the aim of utilizing what little remained locked up in the polar caps. Then, through scientific development, they discovered how to make water – possibly in the same way that we have learned to make synthetic goods to replace natural ones in short supply. It was then an easy matter for them to fill their canals . . . and irrigate as much land as they pleased. I have no doubt, of course, that the supply from the Poles is used as well, otherwise there would be no sensible reason for continuing to use the canals as waterways, as the Martians are seen to do.'

Struggling manfully to put over his questions with pencil and paper Allingham also managed to elicit that the Martians regularly exchanged flying saucer visits with the Venusians and spacemen of both planets were accustomed to landing on the moon. By now it was growing dusk and it was obvious that the conversation could not continue much longer. At this point Allingham remembered that he still had the camera dangling from his neck. He indicated that he would like to take some shots of the saucer resting about twenty yards away and was courteously given permission.

Then the Martian indicated that it was time he was away and motioned Allingham to stand back while he himself got aboard. The sliding panel opened again and the Martian went through it and disappeared from view. But not before Allingham managed to take a quick snap of his retreating back.

Unfortunately he was not near enough to catch so much as a glimpse of the interior of the saucer. The humming noise began again, scarcely louder than the buzz of a fly. Slowly the saucer lifted itself into the air, the dome above the flange revolving swiftly but almost silently, and gradually the wonderful craft glided away – gently at first and then, when it reached an altitude of perhaps forty feet, at tremendous speed. It disappeared into the heavens still heading north. For a while Allingham stared at where it had been, but nothing caught his eye except a few wheeling birds and patches of cloud.

He looked at his watch. It was four twenty-five. 'The whole of that marvellous interview had taken place in half an hour or so; it seemed only a few moments since I had first seen the saucer gliding in across the blue-grey sea, but in this short period I had learned things which scientists had been trying to learn ever since the days of Aristotle.'

Walking thoughtfully back to his caravan, Allingham said, he realized suddenly that it was going to be very difficult to convince anyone of what had taken place. Who would believe his unsupported testimony? Even photographs could be faked. But he decided that if the photographs were any good he would risk it and tell the story in full – to the whole world. Otherwise only a few selected people who could make use of the information he had obtained would get to hear about it. But luck was with Allingham. Suddenly on the road to Lossiemouth he saw a man approaching and recognized him as a fisherman he had seen only a short time earlier.

'To my surprise and great joy,' he recorded later, 'he told me he had seen the saucer and the last few minutes of my meeting with its occupant. He had not at once been able to make up his mind that it was in fact a saucer – it was resting about 500 yards from him when he saw it – but he told me that, from the vantage-point of a nearby hill (whence he had just descended), he had seen it take off and had thus come to the only conclusion possible.'

The man said his name was James Duncan and readily agreed to write a statement that would support anything that Allingham decided to publish about the flying saucer from Mars. It went thus: 'I solemnly swear that between 4.0 p.m. and 4.15 p.m. on the 18th February, 1954, I witnessed a conversation between Cedric Allingham and a man who was the pilot of a flying saucer which landed near Lossiemouth in the county of Moray. Afterwards I saw the pilot get back into the saucer which took off and headed north.'

Cedric Allingham's story was published in book form under the title *Flying Saucer from Mars*. It caused a sensation and, I am told, sold thousands of copies. As science correspondent of the London *Evening News* I received an advance copy for review and read it with increasing astonishment. It was not the first book of its kind. Already Adamski's *Flying Saucers Have Landed* had become a best seller and, if greeted with sceptism in many quarters, had yet to be proved anything but the true experience recorded by an honest man. So there was at least a precedent for claiming to have made contact with someone from another world.

But most reviewers of *Flying Saucers from Mars*, were pretty scornful of Allingham's claim. I was myself. It seemed indeed a likely story! Somehow one just could not imagine anyone behaving in the way Allingham did although, at the same time, it was difficult to imagine how else he might have behaved other than bolting from the saucer in sheer fright. What I instinctively felt was wrong was that the whole interview seemed to have been conducted on too terrestrial terms. For example: it presupposed that the Martians knew that earthmen had been bothered about the Martian 'canals' from the time the Italian astronomer Schiaparelli had first observed them (or thought he had observed them) at his Milan observatory in 1877. And the space visitor, it seemed to me, had behaved in such a matter-of-fact manner as if landing on the Earth were a commonplace activity for such as he. If this were true why had not he or someone like him been seen before in some less remote place than the coast of Morayshire? It really seemed too much to swallow that he would have known about Cedric Allingham and singled him out for the purpose of making contact – for the first time in the history of creation. And what I found more perplexing was why, since he had behaved with such admirable presence of mind in the face of a world-shaking confrontation, had Allingham not managed to get a better picture of the Martian?

The one published showed the hazy backview of someone in the middle distance walking away from the camera, who admittedly *might* have been a man from Mars but could equally well have been a man from Margate. As for the saucer pictures, they could have been genuine; but equally well they could have been faked. One pictured something too high in the sky for clear identification and the others, though conforming to the by now classic Adamski saucer shape, could easily have been 'mocked up'.

In an effort to find out the truth of the matter I tried along with other newspaper men, to locate Cedric Allingham and question him. It should have been easy. Authors who have just published sensational books are not normally reticent – publishers do not allow them to be. Mostly they are only too anxious to come forward. Cocktail parties are arranged for the specific purpose of introducing them to the Press. But not so in the case of Cedric Allingham.

Mind you there was an extenuating circumstance. In the text of his report on the Flying Saucer from Mars he had clearly stated that he had been ill, TB being implied – was not that the reason for his holiday in Scotland? And now his publishers said his condition had worsened and that he had gone abroad to recover. Before long, indeed, it was reported that he was 'dead'.

So that was that. But just a minute. What about the witness James Duncan who had provided in his own handwriting a statement that he also had seen not only the saucer but Allingham talking to a man who later boarded the saucer and took off into the heavens? Surely he could be located? It did not take Fleet Street long to realize this. But once again investigators came up against a blank wall. James Duncan just could not be found.

We had to face, with its disagreeable implications, the fact that James Duncan did not exist. If he did not exist, then the document that purported to be a sworn statement that he, too, had seen the flying saucer, was bogus; and if that were bogus the whole of Cedric Allingham's story must be regarded with deep suspicion.

It all happened (or did not happen) a long time ago and I am not disposed to take a high moral attitude about the matter now. I remember thinking at the time that if Cedric Allingham had made up the entire story and faked not only the statement but the UFO pictures as well, he must have been pretty desperate for money – not apparently that it had done him much good when he got it.

An alternative idea was that if there were no James Duncan and no visitor from Mars, perhaps there was no Cedric Allingham either, despite the photograph in the book purporting to depict him. It was all very strange. Adamski had certainly not hesitated to show himself, but Allingham was being quite exaordinarily backward in coming forward. To the best of my knowledge none of my newspaper colleagues ever succeeded in tracking him down although I heard long afterwards that a man claiming to be the author had, at one time, been persuaded to lecture to a flying saucer club in Sussex.

In view of all the circumstances it might be objected that the story of the flying saucer from Mars has no place in a book aimed at a serious examination of UFO phenomena. But since, over the years, hoaxes have played no insignificant part in the saucer saga I think it would have been wrong to omit what was probably the biggest UFO leg-pull ever perpetrated in Britain.

I am certain in my own mind that Cedric Allingham, if an author of that name ever really existed, did *not* have the experience he claimed – or anything like it. As for his 'death' in Switzerland, I suggest this was no more than a device to put an end to inquiries for him.

In my view, there is a strong likelihood that 'Cedric Allingham' is still alive, in excellent health and far from repentant at having pulled a fast one on thousands of credulous saucerers.

11

Saucers and Flying Ants

The trouble with many attempts to explain away UFO sightings is that the explanations themselves are as far fetched, if not more so, than the actual sightings. In this category I would unhesitatingly put Angus Brooks' experience, which I shall refer to again presently. But sometimes the explanation is so obviously correct that no shadow of doubt remains. A classic example of this concerns the saucer photographed by Mrs Joan Oldfield of Helmshore, Lancs, on an air trip from Manchester to Southampton in March 1966.

Mrs Oldfield and her husband Tom were passengers on a British United Airways Elizabethan airliner flying at 270 miles an hour over Cannock in Staffordshire. It was just after 8 a.m. on a bright sunny morning and the aircraft was flying at 9,000 feet. The Oldfields were on their way to say good-bye to Mrs Oldfield's mother who was about to emigrate to Australia. They had with them a Japanese cine camera.

The aircraft had been airborne about fifteen minutes when Mrs Oldfield, glancing out of a window, saw what she at first took to be a small jet plane following the Elizabethan. She picked up the cine camera from Mr Oldfield's knees and aimed it out of the window. What made her think the craft was a jet was the fact that it was obviously travelling at great speed. Otherwise it was unlike any flying vehicle she had ever seen. It was rather like a short fat cigar with fins and its behaviour was rather strange. After dogging the Elizabethan for a few seconds it seemed to draw in the fins and bank away, and a moment later it had disappeared.

After the Oldfields had had the film developed they ran it through in their cottage on the Lancashire moors and found they had 160 colour frames featuring the UFO and representing seven seconds of viewing time. Their story, including shots from the film became a Sunday newspaper 'splash'. It seemed that here at last was irrefutable evidence that flying saucers really did exist. The film evidence would surely stand up to the harshest inquisition. The UFO could so clearly be seen buzzing around the tail of the Elizabethan and then, so to speak, buzzing off into oblivion.

The film was soon being studied by Defence experts but it was the BBC's 'Tomorrow's World' team which solved the mystery. To do so, they retraced Mrs Oldfield's flight, taking the same pictures from the same seat – and proved conclusively that the flying saucer was no more than a distorted reflection of the aircraft's tail unit. The man who reconstructed the sighting was Francis Greene, nephew of the former BBC Director-General, Sir Hugh Carlton Greene.

It was a splendid piece of detective work and a model for all UFO investigators. To explain away a saucer sighting, Mr Greene showed, the proper thing to do is to reproduce it and show that you can do so over and over again if required to. If all UFO sightings could be dealt with in this way the whole saucer mystery might have been explained away years ago.

The natural and sensible thing to do when presented with UFO phenomena (strange lights in the sky, odd aerial shapes and unusual noises) is to try and explain them in familiar terms. Only when all other possibilities have been explored is it reasonable to turn to extra-terrestrial ideas. We may have reason to *suspect* that there are other worlds supporting civilizations more advanced than ourselves and capable of spying on us across the oceans of space, but we do not *know* this is true.

It is necessary also to keep in mind that there is much about our own world, even about ourselves, that we do not properly understand and which could give rise to sightings. The Defence Ministry investigators who visited Mr Angus Brooks were therefore perfectly justified in their efforts to find a rational explanation for the sighting he reported.

But even supposing they were convinced in their own minds that what Mr Brooks said he saw was in fact a strange flying machine, it is difficult to see how they could have admitted this without causing national, if not world-wide consternation. Imagine the public reaction. Even a casual announcement that the sighting was of some earthly but unknown aircraft would have caused trouble enough. Whose aircraft? Where from? Russia? China? What about our aerial defences? Had everybody been asleep in that they had let in a flying machine from a foreign country? What was it doing here anyway?

The mere suggestion, on the other hand, that the thing may not have come from this world at all, would have had fantastic repercussions. So it was finally admitted! Flying saucers were real – in the sense that they were flying machines from Mars, Venus or some other place. And if this sighting were proved to be of a real flying saucer, what about all the others that had been denied for so long? What the hell was going on? For the officials, who probably would not have known what was going on any more than the rest of us, this would have created quite a dilemma. Better by far to stick to the first principles and knock the thing on the head by any means possible, at least until tangible evidence came to hand.

This is not to say, of course, that the 'floater' suggestion is not a very good one for explaining UFO sightings. But let us examine it more closely. 'Floaters' or 'muscae volitantes' are spots before the eyes; pretty commonplace phenomena, not particularly related to a hang-over, but noticed by people of all ages. Look at a blank space, a ceiling or a window against the sky. Move your eyes a little and there they are drifting across the field of vision: some like tiny tadpoles, others resembling strings of beads, still more appearing as isolated rings.

It used to be thought that these 'spots' were caused by incredibly small dust particles or cellular debris floating on the thin film of liquid coating the eyeball, but further investigation led to the conclusion that they were not on the surface at all but drifting in the transparent semi-fluid, known as vitreous humour, that fills the globe of the eye. They are certainly of cellular origin. Light entering through the cornea (or lens) casts shadows of them on the retina – the sensitive screen at the back of the eye which transforms light energy into nerve impulses for the brain.

The point to be made here, of course, is that most of us have these spots before the eyes and, even without knowing precisely what they are, manage *not* to mistake them for UFOs. Mr Brooks does not think he made that mistake either. In the first place he claims to have observed his UFO for twenty minutes or so, more than enough time for him to have identified it as a floater if such were the case. Besides it did not behave like a floater. It did not simply drift across his field of view, but performed a clear cut manoeuvre that entailed adjustments to its own structure.

The suggestion that the floater may have triggered off a particularly vivid dream is also inclined to strain the imagination. Although it is a commonplace in fiction for an overwrought person to have difficulty in distinguishing between dreams and reality, it is certainly not a problem for most of us in real life. We know very well whether we have been asleep or not and seldom if ever confuse a dream with something that really happened.

In any case why should Mr Brooks have fallen asleep on Moigne Down? He might have done so on a hot afternoon but he is hardly likely to have dropped off (especially without knowing it) on a cold and blustery morning with an alsatian urging him to get up and carry on his journey. What it all boils down to is that the floater explanation might do very well for some UFO sightings – though I do not know whether it has ever seriously been put forward before – but it certainly makes an ineffective show in the case of Mr Angus Brooks.

Many UFO sightings have been explained away as balloons, especially those sent aloft for meteorological purposes. I remember a sunny morning some years ago when hundreds of people telephoned the newspaper for which I was then working to say they had seen a flying saucer over London. This saucer was pretty easily identified as a weather balloon.

Scores of these balloons carrying instruments to measure wind velocity and temperatures are released all over the world every day and not a few are 'lost' in the sense that, having released their instrument packages to float down on parachutes, they drift far from the original areas, buffeted about by upper atmosphere gales. No doubt many of these balloons assume bizarre shapes and reflect the sun's rays in a way that can easily lead to mistakes over their true identity. But, in general, a drifting balloon will normally behave like a drifting balloon. Its movements are sluggish and without purpose.

Thus, as in the case of the West Malling incident, should an alleged 'balloon' behave differently by shooting overhead at a very high speed and disappearing, the observers, especially if they are trained men, may be pardoned for thinking that perhaps it is not a balloon at all. One cannot help thinking indeed that weather balloons provide a very convenient explanation for authorities who have insufficient information, who are frankly baffled or who cannot be bothered to investigate UFO sightings.

No less convenient is the planet Venus, which from time to time shines with exceptional brightness in the night sky and, as in the case of the Flying Cross, is apt to be named as the culprit whenever it happens to be on view and there are no balloons about. However, a great many people over long ages have seen Venus shining brightly without jumping to the conclusion that it is anything other than a planet of the solar system ornamenting the heavens just like a morning or evening star.

One way and another, attempts to rationalize flying saucers have produced some pretty way-out ideas concerning what they are and where they come from. How about this, for example? Saucers are simply clouds of shining phosphorescent organisms from the sea. What happens, according to this notion, is that turbulence in the sea causes a whirling vortex which the wind skims off the surface and carries aloft spinning like a catherine wheel. With the wind behind it, the sea-saucer hurtles through the sky to the amazement of beholders. Certainly it is an idea worth looking into. A film of a 'saucer' forming like this might be of great value in UFO research and might eliminate a number of sightings in coastal areas. But it is difficult to believe that a 'saucer' of such flimsy structure could survive a long inland journey.

A similar idea, by the way, has been put forward in America by Mr Norton Novitt, an amateur scientist of Denver, Colorado; only, instead of marine organisms, the 'saucers' he postulates are made up of swarming insects – flying ants glowing with static electricity. Mr Novitt first became interested in the flying ant theory as a member of the 'moonwatch' team recruited by the US National Aeronautics and Space Administration to make visual observations of large artificial satellites passing overhead. Novitt had set up his telescope to see if he could spot any satellites in daytime. The first object he picked up was a bright spot travelling too fast to be a satellite.

As he watched, a second bright spot joined the first, then both began to descend. Novitt followed them with his telescope until they reached the ground. He could not see them on the ground, but was rather startled to realize that the landing site he was viewing through the telescope was in front of a garage only a short distance away. Puzzled, he went forward to inspect the area and found two winged ants which had apparently just come down from a ritual mating flight. It was sunlight on their bodies, he deduced, that had produced those bright spots in the sky.

The incident led Novitt to read up on the habits of ants. He discovered that many breeds of these insects soar off once or twice a year in mating flights and that some swarms might contain several million insects. What would such swarms look like at night if they could glow? Big luminous blobs wheeling about in the darkened sky like UFOs in many sighting reports. Ants did not normally glow, however – unless they could pick up static electricity from the atmosphere.

As an experiment, Novitt collected several dozen winged ants, glued them to a ping-pong ball and attached the ball by a thin wire to a static generator of the kind used in school demonstrations of electric charges.

When he cranked the generator in a darkened room, the bodies of the ants began to glow, creating dozens of points of light on the surface of the ball. This was fine, except that under normal circumstances the ants would not be connected to a generator. Further inquiries, however, elicited a promising fact. It appeared that ants had a predilection for swarming after a thunderstorm when the air would be heavily charged with electricity. There was also indeed the possibility that they could create their own static charge by rubbing against each other in flight, in much the same way as we ourselves can build up a potential by scuffing our feet across a carpet – and feeling the result as soon as we touch a metal doorknob.

The insect theory is again quite a good one, although one wonders how long the charge on a swarm of flying ants would last, however they acquired it. But it cannot be anything more than a theory until someone establishes that it actually works. What is needed indeed is the capture of an object thought to be a UFO and the discovery that it is in fact a swarm of flying ants. Two ants, as in Novitt's original observation, hardly seems enough to justify the theory.

It is reasonable to suppose that quite a lot of UFO sightings can be attributed to defunct artificial satellites and spent rockets burning up through friction as they plunge back into the atmosphere. Blazing meteorites are probably responsible for a good few more.

In this connection it is perhaps worth recalling that no entirely satisfactory explanation has yet been found for the 'meteorite' that flattened thousands of square miles of Siberian forest land out of existence in 1908. Almost the only certainty, in fact, is that it was not a meteorite. It might have been a comet, but speculation has also included the possibility, however remote, that the damage might have been done by an atomic powered space ship from another world which blew up on entering the earth's atmosphere.

The explosion occurred in such a remote area of the Soviet Union that it was years before any attempt was made to investigate it scientifically. Until Leonid Kulik of the Leningrad Mineralogical Museum raised the money for an expedition in 1921, the only information available consisted of vague word-of-mouth reports from hunters, herdsmen and farmers in the vicinity of Vanavara, an outback trading post.

The reports unanimously referred to a colossal explosion on 30 June 1908. On that summer's day of blue skies and pine-scented air there had been hardly a sound as people at the trading post went peacefully about their business. Then suddenly a blinding ball of fire was seen streaking across the horizon to disintegrate in a mushroom cloud with the thunderous sound of an artillery barrage. A moment later people more than twenty miles away were cowering under the onslaught of a blast that felled trees, shattered windows and ripped the roofs off houses. The shock wave was later learned to have gone twice round the world, and for several nights afterwards many countries had brilliant sunsets and dazzling dawn displays.

Kulik's expedition, although collecting plenty of hearsay evidence to confirm that an explosion had actually taken place, was unable at that time to pinpoint the site of the explosion. It was not until six years later than Kulik, having climbed to the summit of Mount Shakhorma, looked down on a scene of fantastic devastation. For something like six thousand square miles around the Tunguska River an area once covered with majestic firs and pines, not a tree remained standing.

But the strange thing was that their trunks all lay like spokes of a wheel radiating from the same central point. Kulik, without any knowledge of atomic energy or space flight, attributed the devastation to the fall of a giant meteorite, despite the fact that no meteorite particles could be found either at the point of impact or elsewhere in the area.

For many years the Tungus explosion remained an event of only academic interest, but after the atomic bomb explosions at Hiroshima and Nagasaki, Soviet scientists began to look into it with fresh interest. Nothing, many of them felt, fitted the facts of the explosion better than the notion that it was of nuclear origin. The difficulty, however, was that in 1908 destructive atomic energy was unknown and it was unthinkable that an atomic explosion could have occurred naturally.

Was there any other possibility ? One idea put forward was that Siberia might have been hit by a lump of anti-matter from far out in space. Anti-matter being the exact opposite to ordinary matter, would, it was thought, explode with unimaginable force on entering the atmosphere. The trouble was, however, that nobody could be *sure* that anti-matter existed in any quantity anywhere in the universe.

The best rational explanation is that the explosion was caused by a small comet streaking down on Siberia. A comet would undoubtedly explode violently and could well have caused the damage, but would it have laid the trees out in that precise radial display ? Many scientists felt that they would have fallen in a more higgledy-piggledy fashion. Alexander Kazantsev, a Russian scientist who has written copiously about the Tungus mystery, still appears to favour the notion that the explosion was due to an alien spacecraft which ran into trouble and blew up in the atmosphere.

Among other curious features of the event, as he points out, is the fact that there appears to be an odd conflict of evidence concerning the precise way in which the fireball moved in the atmosphere, suggesting that it *may* have changed course. To do so, of course, it would have to be under control.

One explanation for UFOs, against which we appear, thank goodness, to have turned our backs, is that they are generated by fear – mainly fear of the mighty Russian nation. No less a person than Carl Gustav Jung, the great Swiss psychologist, was a protagonist of this idea. In a book published ten years ago, Jung argued that the Communist threat of world domination, leading to an arms race of H bombs and ballistic missiles, had made millions of people so jittery that they were seeing things that just were not there.

Feeling frightened and helpless, they were looking to the heavens for guidance, as they had done down the ages, and were convincing themselves that they could see either warnings or symbols of hope. This, suggested Jung, was the true explanation for most of the mysterious lights seen in the night sky, the hovering spheres and other UFOs. People wanted to believe in messengers from other worlds who might be on their way to prevent a disastrous third world war.

The spate of UFO sightings in the post-war years, said Jung, was not without precedent. Similar visions had been reported throughout history at times of widespread uncertainty and fear. Take, for example, the 'Angels of Mons' – soldiers in the sky that thousands of British, French and American people believed had turned up to help the Allies prevent German advances. In a technological age, it is not angels that appear but mechanical contrivances such as space ships of one sort or another.

As the psychologist put it: 'We have . . . a golden opportunity to see how a legend is formed and how in a difficult and dark time for humanity a miraculous tale grows up of an attempted intervention by extra-terrestrial "heavenly" powers.'

This may well have seemed true at the time it was written but I doubt whether many people, especially in Britain, would go along with it now. The world may not be in a perfect state but we have grown to accept it as it is. We have learned to live with rockets and missiles and, despite the Czechoslovakian trouble, there is probably a better understanding between the great powers of East and West than at any time since the Russian revolution.

But still the saucers come, and although a great many are easily explained away, there is a growing number that stubbornly resist being contemptuously 'shot down'.

12

Where do they come from if . . .

If UFOs are extra-terrestrial, and this is something one is bound to consider once other attempts to explain them have failed, then the question is: 'Where do they come from?'

The universe is unimaginably vast and it might be argued that they could come from almost any part of it; but assuming they have to obey the same physical laws that limit the activities of humanity, the problem is immediately reduced in size. Time and distance, for example, put up formidable opposition to the notion that UFOs, if they *are* indeed piloted spacecraft from other worlds, come from outside the solar system.

Apart from the sun, the nearest star to Earth in the vast galaxy called the Milky Way is Alpha Centauri which is something like four and a quarter light years away. This means that an object leaving the vicinity of Alpha Centauri and heading for Earth at the stupendous speed of light (186,000 miles a second), would still take four and a quarter years to get here and another four and a quarter years to return home. This is a large chunk out of anyone's life, and not one which *we* would care to sacrifice in unrelieved space travel.

Constantly surprised as we are by our own technological miracles, it is not difficult, however, to imagine a race of super-beings who, having conquered death from natural causes and enjoying a life-span of 1,000 years, might not find a ten-year round trip quite so objectionable. One could speculate that, having put their spaceship on course, they relapse into a state of suspended animation to escape the tedium of the greater part of the journey.

It is certainly not too fantastic a notion, especially since earth scientists themselves are dabbling in the techniques of hypothermia to preserve people in unconsciousness for long periods while at the same time they urgently seek an answer to the riddle of ageing.

But before going really way out on this possibility, it is

better perhaps to consider if there may not be a simpler answer to the problem. The earth is not the only planet in our solar system, though it is the only one we know for certain to be inhabited. There are also Mercury, Venus, Mars, Jupiter, Saturn, Uranus, Neptune and Pluto. Astronomers are even beginning to suspect that there may be one more somewhere out beyond the orbit of Pluto. Eight other planets exist which *might* conceivably be 'home' to our visitors from space – to say nothing of the moon and a selection of other natural satellites.

What do we know of them? The answer is that, in general, we know quite a lot but, when it comes to details, not very much. All our observations, except those made by remotely controlling space probes, have had to be made by telescope. We have been peering up through the turbulent atmosphere rather like creatures at the bottom of a pond trying to discover what is going on up in the air and on the surrounding land. One can imagine what a distorted view a fish might have of birds flying overhead, even of ducks swimming on the surface, to say nothing of human beings glimpsed at the water's edge and of tree branches waving in the wind.

The atmosphere which causes stars to twinkle at night distorts our view of everything in the heavens, and when we consider that all our conclusions about other planets in the solar system are based on deductions made over distances of millions of miles, it takes a pretty confident, not to say stubborn, observer to aver that every conclusion is correct.

There are, however, some rules that it seems not unreasonable to apply in determining the general likelihood or otherwise of other planets being able to support life as we know it. All life on earth depends on the sun which coaxed it out of the sea in the first place and now keeps it supplied with energy; it therefore seems pretty safe to assume that life *as we know it* cannot exist on planets which are too far away from the sun to benefit from its light and warmth. Then there would only remain the possibility of life as we do not know it, and this is considered elsewhere.

For the time being it seems that we are obliged to rule out, as too cold, Jupiter, Saturn, Uranus, Neptune and Pluto, leaving Mercury, Venus and Mars. But Mercury would seem to be too close to the sun and therefore too hot for life as we know it. In fact the only two planets worth considering, if we hope to find creatures anything like those which are found on earth, are Venus and Mars, and of these two Mars probably has the edge on Venus as a possible other world.

The Red Planet has indeed been tantalizing humanity for generations – especially since 1877, when the Italian astronomer, Giovanni Schiaparelli, stood back from his telescope at the Milan Observatory and pronounced that one word 'canali'. Schiaparelli had been looking through his telescope at the planet Mars when he noticed what appeared to be faint lines across the surface. Although the lines were on the hazy limit of visibility he was sure they were there, but he did not attempt to draw any specific conclusion from them. In Italian the word he used to describe them meant channels, grooves, crevices – or canals. It was all the same to the astronomer; he was only concerned with making out a scientific report.

But the translation the world seized on was 'canals', for canals did not occur naturally, they had to be dug. That meant someone had dug them, and that meant Mars was inhabited – perhaps by creatures not unlike ourselves.

The canals made a particularly resounding impact on America, where Percival Lowell began to study them and to report many more lines with small round dots at their points of intersection. He was convinced they were the work of intelligent beings who had constructed them to irrigate a drought-stricken planet. But Mars continued to be a very long way away – it never comes nearer than about thirty-five million miles – and public interest soon subsided. So nobody was very disappointed when a French astronomer Eugène Antoniadi concluded in 1929 that the canals were simply optical illusions created by the immense distance over which they were being viewed.

From observations over the years, astronomers have nevertheless built up a pretty comprehensive picture of Mars, a picture of a world which from a distance appears to bear a remarkable likeness to our own world, although it is only about half the size, and which pursues a similar course round the sun, turning on its own axis once every twenty-four hours thirty-seven minutes.

But a year on Mars lasts 687 days, this being the time it takes to get once round the sun, and consequently the seasons are much longer. Mars certainly has an atmosphere. This has been deduced from drifting cloud formations which also indicate that Martian winds blow up to sixty miles an hour. Clearly visible are the polar caps which expand and shrink rhythmically in accordance with seasonal changes. What else but snow or ice crystals?

Two-thirds of the planet's surface are a rosy-orange colour (hence the nickname Red Planet), and these two-thirds are presumably desert. There are also dark belts which change colour from time to time, indicating vegetation of a sort. For many years it was held that this vegetation could be nothing more than lichen, able to survive the extremes of Martian temperature, but a new theory put forward by Russian scientists is that much of the vegetation could be bigger plants of the cacti class. This theory is based on a careful analysis of light reflected by cacti in desert areas on earth and on a comparison of it with a similar analysis of light from the dark areas of Mars. But nobody really knows and nobody will know until man sets foot on the Red Planet and finds out at first hand.

Another conclusion drawn, and one which supports the old canal idea, is that Mars has no seas; otherwise, astronomers say, the sun's rays would be reflected from them.

Mars, of course, has already had a visitor from Earth. The visitor was America's Mariner 4, the remarkable robot cameraman which flew past the Red Planet in July 1965. But what did Mariner 4's snapshots, later televised to Earth, really tell us about Mars? Precious little.

This is not to denigrate an historic technical feat. Mariner 4 travelled for eight months through empty space to take those pictures under radio guidance from Earth and behaved impeccably; but the fact remains that the robot was never nearer the planet's surface than 6,000 miles. And all these pictures showed, in the final analysis, was a cratered surface similar to that of the moon with mountain ranges that *might* account for the 'canal' markings but equally well might not.

The pictures revealed nothing that might indicate either the presence of intelligent life, unintelligent life or even the presence of vegetation. There just was not sufficient clarity to bring out such details. Indeed one could easily conclude from the pictures that Mars was as barren as the moon appears to be. A bald, rocky, airless world. Except that we know this is not so. Other clues indicate that Mars is on a much higher evolutionary plane than the moon. And, as has often been pointed out since, pictures taken by Tiros weather satellites in orbit round the Earth show much the same barrenness from an altitude of only a few hundred miles. Looking at the Tiros pictures, indeed, one could be pardoned for assuming that the earth itself was uninhabited and devoid of vegetation, even of water.

In other words, whatever other scientific value they may have, the pictures televised by Mariner 4 cannot be accepted as giving any kind of proof that there is life on Mars or otherwise. However, it seems likely that the matter will be resolved before long; for although a journey to Mars and back would take something like eighteen months this is not an entirely unendurable period for trained men. Both Russia and America, indeed, have plans for manned journeys to Mars once the moon has been explored.

In the meantime, more and more probes will be sent to the Red Planet, probes of increasing sophistication which can be soft landed and instructed by radio to send back information about the terrain, temperature and atmosphere. The Americans also hope to get close-up pictures of the two baby moons of Mars, Deimos and Phobos, particularly the latter. Phobos, about ten miles in diameter, is intriguing because of the precise way in which it orbits the Martian equator, maintaining an almost perfect circle. Its behaviour has led Soviet scientists to speculate that it just might be an artificial satellite. Should close-up pictures reveal features indicating that Phobos is artificial, one can imagine the excitement this could cause. The finding could only mean that Mars is or has been inhabitated by intelligent beings.

The Americans are pinning their hopes of finding out about Phobos on two new Mariner probes, bigger and better than Mariner 4, scheduled for launching in 1971. These robots are to fly past the Red Planet at an altitude of about 2,000 miles but they will also be carrying much more powerful cameras than Mariner 4, cameras that could produce pictures equivalent in clarity to a naked eye view of the surface from between 3,000 to three hundred feet.

Altogether the Americans hope to get back a minimum of sixty-six TV pictures from the twin probes. Each will be instructed to take eight approach shots and twenty-five fly-by close-ups. It is in the approach shots that the scientists hope Phobos, if not Deimos as well, will show up.

VENUS

On the face of it there is not much to be said for Venus as the home of UFOs. Not, at any rate, if one judges entirely from information radioed back to earth by the two space probes, one Russian and one American, sent to the planet in 1967. The probes, Mariner 5 and Venus 4, arrived in the vicinity of Venus in October that year after a four months space journey.

Mariner 5 flew on past the planet at an altitude of 2,000 miles and, after sending back particulars concerning temperatures, density and magnetic field, became a small satellite of the sun. Venus 4 played a much more dramatic role. Instead of simply observing the planet from a distance, the probe released a tiny automatic radio station which floated down through the atmosphere and actually landed on the surface of the planet. It was an incredible feat of technology. The radio operated for only a few hours while its batteries lasted, but in that time the Russians got back a great deal of valuable information from it.

They learned, for example, that the atmosphere of Venus is fifteen times denser than that of earth, largely composed of carbonic acid, and that the surface temperature goes up to 500° F. But whereas the American probe detected a weak magnetic field there was no evidence of this in any message from Venus 4.

In piecing together what had been learned from both robots, American and Russian scientists agreed that life on Venus was quite impossible. Dr Von R. Eshleman, a Stanford University physicist, said the planet was 'not just like hell – it's like a hell-hole'. The dreadful heat, he said, was built up in much the same way as in a greenhouse. The rays of the sun having penetrated the planet's thick cloud cover, are trapped as if under glass. But the heat is too awful even for the most heat-loving tropical plants to flourish in it. What is more, said Dr Eshleman, the atmosphere density would produce fantastic optical illusions so that 'it would take a long time for people living there – if there were any – to realize they were on a spherical planet. The horizon would always appear high, giving the person the impression that he was living in the bottom of a bowl.'

At sunset, he suggested, the sun would not go down in the normal way, but would appear to diffuse along the horizon, so that night would still be illuminated by a distorted reflection of the sun as a glowing ribbon of light until, at sunrise – 117 earth days later – it would reassemble in the west. Theoretically, it would be possible for a man standing on Venus to see the back of his own head. The dense atmosphere would bend the light rays so much that the image would circle the planet.

Reports on data from both probes appeared to have effectively destroyed every science fiction notion of Venus as an habitable planet, although it was only a decade since imaginative writers had thought of the planet, at worst, as a place of steaming swamps populated by prehistoric monsters of a type that once roamed the surface of the earth. Alternatively, instead of swamps and jungles, there might be vast oceans teeming with fish life including perhaps intelligent aquatic mammals.

But this possibility, it now seemed, could be entirely discounted. Venus was more likely to be wholly desert or as hard and barren as the moon. Indeed a later American experiment only served to corroborate this view.

The experiment, carried out by astronomers at Cornell University, was to map the planet's surface from data obtained by probing into the cloud cocoon with a powerful radar beam and analyzing the return signals with the help of a computer. Most of the probing was done during 1964 and 1967, when Venus was as near to Earth as she ever comes – a mere twenty-five million miles away. Afterwards the astronomers started jig-sawing the computer information together to obtain the first rough notion of what Venus really looks like. Having done a third of the surface they reckoned they had a pretty good idea, though by no means a detailed one. The radar signals suggested that the surface of Venus was in fact harder than that of the moon; that most of the northern hemisphere was mountainous while the southern was relatively flat and smooth.

So what was hopefully regarded as Earth's twin, with an estimated diameter of 7,800 miles compared with the earth's 7,926 miles, could apparently be dismissed as nothing of the sort. Yet scientists have not been willing to rule out completely the possibility that life of some sort may have developed there. Dr W. H. Pickering, director of the Jet Propulsion Laboratory at Passadena, has said that there may be 'low forms of life floating in the high altitudes or on extremely high mountains,' and the Soviet scientist Nikolai A. Krasilnikov has suggested that life forms similar to heat resistant microbes found on earth might thrive in the Venusian atmosphere.

But not even these small concessions from orthodox science are likely to commend themselves to those who, wishful thinking perhaps, expected something better of Venus. There is always the escape route provided by the phrase 'life as we know it'. For that is what the scientists mean. But before going into that, there are still one or two more possible 'worlds' to consider.

THE MOON

If not Mars or Venus, is there the slightest chance that flying saucers come from the moon? By comparison, the moon is extremely near to us, a mere quarter of a million miles away and there are many who would rule it out as a place about which we know pretty nearly all there is to know. But is this really true? What about, for example, the mysterious flashes that astronomers have occasionally seen in the craters of the moon? Can we be perfectly certain of what goes on (or does not go on) on the side of the moon which is never turned to us?

Throughout history men have been looking at the moon, speculating about it and weaving fancies. The primitive savage, crouching at the mouth of his cave, gazed up in wonderment. Perhaps his first sense of beauty was aroused in this contemplation. And then, as ages rolled by, the moon played an ever increasing part in the affairs of men. Ritual murder was committed by moonlight. Attacking armies waited for the full moon before descending on their unsuspecting neighbours.

Sailors looked to the moon to guide them in choosing tides and plotting their way across uncharted seas. Musicians sang to it and poets praised it. Lovers basked in its reflected radiance and inexplicable madness was attributed (quite wrongly) to its influence.

But all the time astronomers were learning more and more about the moon. They realized it was another world and their telescopes revealed that what was superstitiously believed to be the face of the Man in the Moon was in fact the outline of mountain ranges.

Now, with powerful modern telescopes, we can see the moon's surface, clearly enough to make pretty accurate maps of it, to count and classify the thousands of craters with which it is pitted. Both Russia and America have put 'spy' satellites into orbit round the moon. Both, in addition, have landed remote controlled space vehicles on the moon's surface to take photographs in their immediate vicinity, examine the surface and test the strength of it for landing still bigger vehicles. American astronauts have orbited the moon and the landing of a manned space ship is imminent. By the end of the decade, indeed, it may well be that we shall have learned all there is to know about the moon; but meanwhile much of our accumulated store of 'knowledge' must be regarded as speculative.

What do we know so far? We know the moon is smaller than the earth and would just about fit into the basin of the Atlantic ocean (from which according to one theory it was originally torn). We know it has lofty mountain ranges, higher even than Mount Everest, and vast plains once thought to be seas but now regarded as lava beds. Pictures from Apollo 8 indicate that the moon is a pretty barren place, a massive ball of bare rock. We know it is silent and eerie with incredible extremes of temperature: blistering heat by day and sub-Arctic cold by night. And we know that a 'day' on the moon lasts a fortnight by our own reckoning and a night the same.

We know there is no atmosphere like the Earth's, and consequently little chance of plant or animal life; and we know the sky is always dark so that stars can still be seen even when the sun is up. We know the moon orbits the Earth roughly once a month and that each time it encircles us it turns once on its own axis – which accounts for the fact that it keeps the same face towards us. Pictures taken of the hidden side of the moon indicate that it is not very different from the side we do see. The surface looks just as bare and cratered.

The moon, indeed, does not seem at all an attractive place to visit, but it must again be pointed out that most of our conclusions have been drawn from a pretty long distance away and nearly all our direct observations made by peering up through the haze of the earth's atmosphere. It seems unlikely that the moon has much to offer in the way of material rewards:

nothing like the varied and fascinating life on earth. But it may not be quite as barren as we now suppose; it may even have an atmosphere, albeit a tenuous one. In recent years astronomers have observed what appear to be mists collecting in some of the craters; others claim to have detected faint lights which they assume to be caused by meteors (shooting stars) catching alight through atmospheric friction as they approach the lunar surface.

If we allow that there may be an atmosphere, can we entirely rule out the possibility of vegetation, and if we allow vegetation, however primitive, can we absolutely rule out all forms of life? In any case, it is as well to remember that we are only dealing with the surface of the moon. What about below the surface? Is it stretching imagination too far to postulate the existence of creatures – big, small, intelligent, unintelligent, you name it – living in vast underground caves?

Admittedly there is more than a touch of science fiction about this. But what of it? Fiction is the result of imagination. Imagination produces theories. Theories lead to exploration and discovery. In this book we are concerned not only with facts, we are also concerned with imagination and theory. As long as we do not know exactly what UFOs may be, we are entitled to enter realms of speculation which many would regard as over-fanciful.

What about, for example, the possibility of the moon, if it is really as barren and unproductive as it looks, being used as a base by beings from other worlds, who have come to see what we are doing on this earth? After all, we ourselves are planning to establish bases on the moon in the next few years so as to make our own exploration of the solar system easier. The moon may not look big in the sky but it is at least a sixth the size of earth – plenty large enough to provide hiding-places for anyone technologically capable of landing on it and wishing to keep out of sight. If there were no lunar caves and they couldn't dig in, there is the whole of the hidden side of the moon to give concealment.

Admittedly there is a kind of wishful thinking about this. We seem to be back with the long-haulers from the neighbourhood of Alpha Centauri and beyond. But one other place in the solar system we have still to consider as a possible place from which UFOs might originate, is – the earth itself. I said in an earlier chapter that UFO sightings had been made throughout recorded history. If this is so UFOs may also have been seen long before men could read and write. Suppose they have always been with us. Suppose it is only in recent times that we have begun to appreciate these phenomena for what they really are. Suppose that existing alongside mankind there has been a different kind of earth creature with a technology infinitely superior to our own, able to control forces that we can scarcely imagine. Suppose we have only just reached the requisite stage in our intellectual development when we can begin to catch glimpses of him and his machines at times when they are off-guardedly visible.

To anyone convinced that humanity has all the answers and has plumbed every secret of the physical universe, this is palpable nonsense. The greater likelihood, however, is that we still have a great deal left to learn. Indeed it is not so much a likelihood as a certainty, for every scientific advance opens up new and staggering vistas for future exploration and achievement. Fly a kite or a balloon – and before long there are supersonic jets hurtling across oceans and continents. Split the atom and the whole concept of atomic energy is revealed. Send a simple radio message and there is television in every home. Fire a rocket and the moon and planets are waiting to be explored. Solve the genetic code and the whole human race may undergo a fundamental change ... In modern parlance it is all happening.

But what if these other earth creatures are not particularly keen to mix with us or share their secrets? What if they are unimaginably old in the evolutionary sense and have so far managed to conceal, except for occasional lapses, the evidence of their development and being? What if they have the ability, as Alan Watts suggests, to generate 'force fields' to deflect radar beams and make themselves literally invisible?

Certainly this is a highly speculative approach to the problem of UFOs but, in the absence of real evidence to explain the phenomena, surely any speculation is permissible; and granted that the possibility is even remotely tenable we have next to ask ourselves where, on earth, do they come from? Nor is it unduly difficult to think up possible answers. People living and working in thickly populated areas, in towns and villages, tend to have a rather restricted view of what this earth is really like. Life to them seems comfortably cut and dried. All is known. There is not a place left on earth where man has not set foot. But you would be surprised. In fact barely a quarter of the earth's surface is well known and much of that has still to be scientifically explored. There are vast tracts of uninhabitated land in the Soviet Union, in China and Tibet, in India, Australia and Africa, in South America, Canada and Alaska, at both the North and the South Poles. They may be frozen, arid and inhospitable areas in which few of us would care to live, but we are not concerned with our own preference or even our own ability to adapt to local conditions. The type of beings we have in mind could presumably have adapted themselves to any conditions – and that includes living under the sea. Three-fifths of the earth's surface is under water and we are only just beginning to explore the depths.

There is a good chance, some would say a very good chance, that scientists will eventually come up with an explanation for UFOs which is perfectly satisfactory in natural, even commonplace terms. The majority, official investigators say, are in fact explained away quite simply. But even if it appears that the world has never been visited by a manned spacecraft or unmanned research probe from elsewhere in the universe, this is not to say it never will be.

The notion that the planet Earth is unique, and humanity the only intelligent creatures in the entire cosmos, is already going by the board. The mathematical improbability of this is overwhelming. Intelligent life, even if it is not life as we know it, must indeed be pretty common if, as astronomers say, there are hundreds of thousands of possibilities for other worlds in our own galaxy alone. The problem from our point of view is how to get in touch with them, if they are not actually trying to get in touch with us. The space probes we have sent to Mars and Venus, though splendid technological achievements for this stage in humanity's evolution, seem woefully inadequate to operate on a universal scale.

In time, of course, we or our descendants will think of something very much better. But what can we do today? Can we do anything? Are we doing anything? In fact we are. We are picking up radio signals that reach us from far out in space. The intensity of this listening is growing as more and more radio sources are discovered and the clamour of the universe grows louder.

Not long ago an editorial in the *New York Times* asked: 'Has man finally made contact with the space communications network of the advanced galactic civilizations whose existence has long been suspected though never demonstrated?'

The question followed the discovery of pulsars, pulsating radio sources, which astronomers nicknamed LGMs for Little Green Men. The strange thing about these pulsars is their power and the regularity of their signals. It seemed at first that such regularity could only indicate a deliberate attempt to attract attention, but then it was realized that the pulsars were radiating in all directions – a terrible waste of energy in communication. They were also signalling over a broad range of frequencies which was also wasteful. So it appeared that after all the LGMs were some sort of natural phenomena.

But the notion of super civilizations cannot easily be laughed off. It is perfectly feasible that at some future time we shall pick up signals from space that are indisputably intended for communication purposes. It may not be for fifty years. On the other hand it may be tomorrow.

Commenting on pulsars in a Soviet newspaper, Academician G. Naan, an eminent Estonian scientist, said: 'Thirty years ago the problem of interplanetary and interstellar communication was regarded as fantastic. Only twenty years ago it was a purely academic problem. Today it has obviously become a practical one. Manned spaceflights have inspired us with confidence that the foreseeable future may really see direct contact between different civilizations.'

When we make contact, will the alien civilization be at a higher or lower stage of development than our own? There are plenty of strong reasons, says Naan, for thinking it 'very unlikely that we shall come into contact with beings who are even more foolish than we are'.

But the really interesting thing about Naan's speculations concerns his views on how alien people may regard us – indeed may already be regarding us. There are three possible attitudes they could adopt, he says. Firstly they may show interest and understanding, wanting to know more and displaying goodwill towards us.

That would seem to be the ideal situation. They would supply us with extremely valuable scientific, technological, artistic and other information, and would warn us against ridiculous or fatal mistakes – say, against ignoring lines of scientific development to which the future belongs and against steps leading to the contamination of the environment or even annihilation.

A second possibility is that the aliens may show understanding but no interest. In this connection he comments: 'If the other civilization were a very long way ahead of us, then it might look upon us in much the same way that we look at ants. What could we teach the ants and what could we warn them against?'

The third possibility is one of interest but no understanding: 'We might interest them only from a purely practical – for instance, gastronomic! – point of view.'

There is the fourth possibility that the aliens would display neither interest nor understanding, but since a civilization which took such an attitude would hardly bother to send out signals in the first place, this can be ignored. What people on earth must do, Naan urges, is develop the proper attitude to space exploration and the probability that contact will be made with other civilizations. If another civilization has the technical means of locating us we will not, in any case, be able to hide.

'When we have established a space contact,' Academician Naan concludes, 'we shall, in all probability, be dealing with highly intelligent beings. The encounter may help us to understand our own position in space, our place on the ladder of cosmic evolution. This is one of the beneficial aspects of discussing space prospects. It makes us take a broader look at things. We are the product of a definite social, biological and cosmic evolution . . . The idea of the absolute superiority of our own stage of evolution – just like everything that is terrestrial and "ours" – is undoubtedly among the most naïve of illusions. The time allocated to us on the cosmic scale is not yet over, for we are as yet so imperfect and are far from having exhausted the possibilities inherent in the social stage of evolution.

In connection with Naan's speculations, it should be borne in mind that any visitors, welcome or otherwise, we may have from other worlds would not necessarily resemble ourselves, even superficially. Indeed, there seems to be more than an even chance of their being as little like us as many of the other creatures (ranging from the ant to the ostrich) which share this earth with humanity. This notion was explored with great good humour at the annual meeting of the British Association for the Advancement of Science in Southampton in 1964. Professor J. T. Williams, professor of botany at Southampton University, delighted a large audience with his ideas about 'men' – or monsters – from outer space who, he said, far from evolving like ourselves, might instead be the products of entirely different life systems. Essentially their bodies might be composed of substances as unlikely (to us) as rock or tin.

For life to continue from one generation to another, said the professor, what was fundamentally required was a chemical compound of sufficient complexity to carry hereditary information, yet so constructed that it could easily be duplicated. We ourselves had a compound of carbon of phosphorus; and although we did not know if any other systems would work, it was possible to conceive of some that *might* work – systems involving, for example, carbon and fluorine, phosphorus and nitrogen or silicon and oxygen.

Creatures depending on such compounds would also need a fluid to make their systems work just as we need water for ours. But in their case the fluid might be liquid ammonia. Professor Williams postulated, for instance, a 'Jupiter man' developing intelligently in oceans of liquid ammonia and being unable to survive outside such an environment. Or what about 'Mercury man' with silicon as his basic ingredient? He would be so hot that water would boil in contact with him; to survive he would require a liquid salt environment. And a 'man' made of phosphorus, nitrogen and chlorine would have to breathe chlorine instead of oxygen.

Professor Williams' ideas were put forward in a light-hearted manner, but the aim was to stimulate the imaginations of young scientists and make them realize that the bug-eyed monsters of science fiction were not entirely preposterous. The point is valid, especially in view of mankind's forthcoming adventures in space, because not the least of our problems in dealing with intelligent creatures, should we meet any, from other parts of the universe, may well be to recognize them as intelligent creatures in the first place.

13
UFOs as a Cult

What if the whole UFO business is no more than a cult, drawing its adherents from people who see in it some vague new form of religion? It is a point to be considered. So let us take a look at ufology in that light and see what we make of it.

In the beginning, at least as far as modern worship of the UFO is concerned, was the announcement by Kenneth Arnold that he had seen a chain of saucer-like things flying near Mount Rainier in June 1947. Flying Saucers! Could it be that this fanciful name established for the first time an identity for a class of phenomena which hitherto people had only dimly been aware of? Could it be that now, for the first time, they could come forward and say: 'Yes, I've seen something like that'.

Certainly it is a fact that from 1947 to 1951 the number of sighting reports continued to grow all over the world until there could hardly have been any adult person in the civilized world who had not heard of flying saucers, even if they did not know what they were. In the following year more than 1,000 sightings were reported in the United States alone.

Then there came a brief lull – at least as far as general public interest was concerned, although UFO sightings continued to be reported, especially from north-west Europe where the biggest flap of all time occurred in 1954, and the French author and UFO investigator, Aimé Michel, published evidence purporting to show that many sightings followed a clear pattern of straight lines across the continent.

But it was not until the launching of Sputnik I in 1957, when people generally had a new reason for looking up at the sky, that UFO reports made a fresh impact on the public Press.

In the meantime a number of books, some of which have already been mentioned, had been published and were being avidly read, especially by those who already had an affinity for the occult. These books, which at the time few other people took seriously, moved the saucer 'cult' into a new phase, for the authors claimed not only to have seen UFOs but to have seen them land and to have spoken to members of the crews and learned that they came from other planets.

Magazines devoted to ufology were also beginning to appear and, as a direct consequence, clubs and organizations concerned with the study of flying saucers were formed and invited the authors to come and give lectures on their 'experiences'. One heard at this time a lot about 'our space brothers', telepathy, force fields and vibrations. The notion was gaining ground that intelligent, indeed *super*-intelligent beings from other worlds were dropping in to warn us of the perils facing us if we did not mend our ways, eschew belligerence and embrace brotherly love.

The concept of flying saucers was no longer a simple matter of trying to explain unidentified objects in the sky; all that was dead and done with. We knew all about the saucers *per se* and it was now a question of trying to apply the wisdom they were prepared to share with us.

An American psychologist writing on the saucer cult at that time, painted a very unflattering picture of the majority of people concerned with it. A survey of UFO clubs, he said, revealed the fact that most members tended to be elderly women, widowed or single. They were generally from the upper working classes or lower middle classes whose standard of education was below average. 'Although they spend their time learning and consider themselves as "students", they do not learn things in an ordered and disciplined way,' he said, 'but build up chunks of knowledge which they cannot bring to bear on a problem and which they cannot systematize.'

In addition, their physical health did not appear to be of the best, quite apart from their high average age. Many members were deaf, many had poor vision, many walked with sticks or had other obvious physical defects. Hallucinations were quite common, though it was accepted among them that 'seeing things' was a mark of special sensitivity.

'If one were to attend a meeting and watch the action without knowing in advance whether the audience was in a mental hospital or not,' the psychologist proclaimed, 'it would be very difficult to tell, because many symptoms of serious illness are displayed . . . Men in the audience tend to be either young schizophrenics or aged with advance senility.'

What kept the flying saucer clubs alive, it was alleged, was that in one way or another they were pitching for a better world with the spiritual alleviation of ill-health and distress – the essential purpose of religions down the ages. When it was published, this analysis certainly had a ring of dismal truth. But if it still applies, it can only do so in a very general sense. What seems clear in the sixties is that the true ufologists have parted company with the crackpots.

Britain's *Flying Saucer Review* certainly does not aim to increase its circulation among the feeble or foolish – they would not be interested. Contributors to the *Review* are serious-minded people, including doctors and scientists, and the sighting reports published are objectively handled to record a mystery that is continuously fascinating to the open-minded.

Mr Charles Bowen, editor of the *Review* since October 1964, puts it like this: 'What we are doing is keeping the record. Some of us may have personal views on the UFO mystery, but the object of the *Review* is to keep readers up-to-date with information that we believe to be factual, and at the same time to carry out investigations we consider worthwhile.'

The *Review's* team of writers and consultants includes scientists such as Dr Jacques Vallée, the French astronomer and computer expert, Mr C. Maxwell Cade, a specialist in radiation medicine, and design engineer, Mr R. H. B. Winder. Others include aeronautics historian, Charles H. Gibbs-Smith, Dr Bernard Finch, Aimé Michel, a French authority on UFOs, Gordon Creighton, ex-diplomat and linguist, and Derek Dempster, an aviation writer and joint author of an authoritative history of the Battle of Britain. In addition the *Review* has correspondents in all parts of the world and is circulated to more than fifty countries where it is read by government departments and learned societies.

Most of the acknowledged experts in saucer research have been sifting evidence for many years and are no less wary of being deceived than the orthodox scientists who take the view that the whole business is a manifestation of human frailty and foolishness. Very few of them have had any personal experience of a sighting, but one who has is Gordon Creighton, who was puzzled by the appearance of an unidentified flying object years before anything about flying saucers began to appear in the popular press. It was during the summer of 1941, while he was serving as First Secretary and Chinese Secretary at the British Embassy in Chungking. He and two fellow diplomats were standing in a garden high up on the south bank of the River Yangtze when they saw a white disc-like object flying very fast over the city from the north-east to the south-west. The object, Mr Creighton recalls, had a bright central light that flashed on and off as it sped across the sky. None of the observers had the slighest idea what it could be and never found out, but, as far as Mr Creighton was concerned, the experience was vivid enough to have a permanent place in his memory and to become one of the foundations of his interest in UFO research.

All serious ufologists admit that by far the largest proportion of sightings in Britain, as elsewhere, can be accounted for by observers' mistakes. So many ordinary aircraft, balloons, birds and insects take to the skies that it is not surprising that under certain circumstances, especially at twilight, people should mistake them for UFOs. In addition there are optical illusions caused by isolated areas of the atmosphere acting as lenses and reflectors and producing distorted images of familiar objects in the vicinity.

But what the ufologists maintain is that, even when all this has been taken into account and appropriate reductions made from the total, there are still more than enough unexplained sightings left to justify scientific investigation. Is it not also possible, they suggest, that some of the explanations which the authorities arrive at so confidently, are just a bit too pat? So an aircraft happens to be in the area in which a sighting is made – right, that's that. But what if the crew of a UFO were using the presence of the aircraft to cover their own activities?

This is not the view of people with obvious physical or mental disabilities. Nor is it the view of elderly folk who, it may be thought, have lost the capacity for logical thinking. It is the view of the young and inquisitive, who are growing ever more impressed with the evidence for the existence of UFOs as mysterious flying machines. I do not belong to any saucer research organisation and have only a mild interest in the occult, but my work over the past fifteen years or so has brought me into contact with many people who believe in UFOs and are prepared to consider the possibility that they are here for some as yet undisclosed purpose. Nor, with few exceptions, does it seem to me that they are any less intelligent (though they may be more imaginative) than those who reject the UFO phenomena out of hand.

Since this purports to be a book of imagination as well as one of analysis, it may be a useful exercise to suppose for a moment that we *are* being visited by beings from space, and to try to examine the situation from their point of view. Why are they here? Why do they behave in such a furtive, not to say idiotic, manner? Is there anything *we* can do to further a better understanding with them? After all this is something people of civilized countries lean over backwards nowadays to try and do among themselves.

Since it would appear that 'they' have a technology vastly superior to ours, it seems reasonable to assume that they are not afraid of us. Then why, instead of clearly revealing themselves to all and sundry, should they only land in remote areas, usually when nobody is about; and then, on the few occasions when they choose to make contact, only appear to the most unlikely representatives of our race? George Adamski was never recognized, even among those who knew him well, as a specially gifted man, nor does it seem that destiny had earmarked Ernest Arthur Bryant for special favours.

Why not pick on a few distinguished statesmen, scientists and religious leaders and invite their co-operation in putting the message over? That is, of course, if in *their opinion* such people are distinguished and right for the job. On the whole, a better idea is that 'they' do not consider we are ready for a total revelation and think that more will be achieved by keeping us guessing. In this case, it could be many years, perhaps even hundreds of years, before the truth about flying saucers becomes known. By then we would have slowly adjusted ourselves to the idea of interplanetary, if not interstellar traffic – not just a few of us, but everybody. And then the revelation, instead of coming as a shock, would be accepted naturally.

Most people who think about it at all accept that there *must* be beings on other worlds, although some may not be in such an advanced state of civilization (if that is the right word) as ourselves; but there must also, on a purely statistical basis, be civilizations vastly superior to our own with technical knowledge we cannot begin to understand. Yet, as Charles Gibbs-Smith pointed out in his letter to *The Times*, this notion is by no means generally accepted. The vast majority of people do not want to know. Their attitude to our own efforts to travel in space is largely one of indifference born of a failure to comprehend its significance.

As for flying saucers – a bit of a joke, you know. Laugh it off. That is the best way of dealing with any concept that seems too complicated or too frightening to become involved with. Yet many of the same people apparently have no difficulty in believing that Jesus Christ fed 5,000 with five loaves and two fishes.

The human brain is the most astonishing instrument in all earthly creation. It is made of billions of parts directly or potentially connected to one another. All the telephone, telegraph, radio and radar apparatus in the world is less intricate than the three pounds of brain matter in a human skull. Quite literally we do not know what we are doing most of the time; the brain does it for us.

Just think of all the detailed adjustments of movement and balance enabling us to run downstairs without falling. Think of what is involved in making the noises we call speech. Think of the way we can learn to use a typewriter, play the piano or drive a car without giving conscious thought to the mechanics of it. Yet every tiny action is the result of a nerve signal controlled by the brain; and when we become tired the brain can switch us off for a few hours to give us – and itself – a rest.

Nobody can construct a human brain. Indeed it has been estimated that to build even a crude model would require 1,000 billion transistors, an equal number of wires, a warehouse thirteen hundred times the size of an average room and at least a million kilowatts of electric power. Yet our brains manage on a mere twenty-five watts, casually carrying out work programmes that would baffle the most elaborate computer in existence.

Nor is the brain solely concerned with what is happening now, but also with what has happened in the past. It has an elaborate storage system that we call memory, though how it works is largely a mystery. Even those of us who complain of having a bad memory may be able to recall experiences dating back half a century. The point is, of course, that we do not really know very much about ourselves and our innate capabilities, particularly why some people should be cleverer than others or more sensitive.

The brain, it has been pointed out, evolved in the first place as a food seeking system and is no more necessarily a truth finding apparatus than the snout of a pig. But it has certainly become adapted, particularly in modern times, to processes of inquiry and analysis. Not everyone, of course, uses his brain in this way and it is significant that we continue to make a distinction between people with 'open minds' and those who, having reached a conclusion, find it impossible to re-examine it in the light of fresh evidence.

But the full use of brain power is essential in this context, because if there is anything in the UFO mystery other than the misinterpretation of familiar objects or the failure to understand certain complexities of the earth's atmosphere, then an imaginative approach to the problem is vital if we are ever going to solve it. Nor is this any less the case should it turn out that the fault is in ourselves rather than in our stars.

Put another way, something is evidently going on in the world which is peculiar to this age, even if it is simply the onset of a strange new malady.

In the context of an imaginative approach, one is justified, I suppose, in postulating the existence of a remarkable Galactic Society entirely composed of super-eggheads which has established itself over the ages, dating back perhaps to long before the first humanoid savage scratched his puzzled head in the flowering wilderness of prehistory. That would give them a pretty good start on us both morally and technically. Heavens, what couldn't they do now! To them, our efforts at space travel would seem hardly less promising of scientific progress than the toilsome journeys of the covered wagons heading West in the nineteenth century. Indeed they would have long forgotten any primitive efforts they may have made themselves to overcome gravity. What was that again? Gravity? Why just press this button . . .

As for hopping around the universe, who said the speed of light imposed any restrictions on space travel? Haven't you heard of inverse-time-photo-whatsitsname? All you do is pick your destination, say 1,000 light-years away, move on to the intergalactic field force and let her go boy! Make it in time for lunch, easy. Tell you what, let's have another look at that planet Earth. They're crazy, man!

It's fun to watch them but you are not supposed to land or make contact (although it has been done once or twice to start them thinking) because the Grand Council reckon they won't be ready for the awful truth for another thousand years. It doesn't matter if they catch a glimpse of the ship; it helps with what the Council call Primary Indoctrination. But mind the radar bit. If they lock on to you they just might start shooting – they're a belligerent lot. Just shift along the spectrum line. If you disappear they'll decide you were never there in the first place. Whatever happens you mustn't risk getting captured or losing the ship or any part of it. The GC would do their nuts about that!

The point I have been trying to make is simply that *if* superior intelligences from other worlds *were* interested in this planet, for whatever reason other than trying to destroy it, the chances are that they would not want to make direct contact. The chances are that they would behave in much the same way as they are behaving – *if they are*. And from our point of view it is worth bearing in mind that it only needs one utterly indisputable, copper-bottomed, stone ginger certainty of a sighting, contact or inter-planetary conversion piece, to vindicate the whole idea of ufology.

Have we had it and failed to recognize it, or have we not had it at all? Let us now look at what may be termed the official view of the phenomena.

14
Official Views

It has been possible in this book to outline only a few of the more dramatic UFO stories related to the British Isles. In fact, as mentioned earlier, the Ministry of Defence looked into a total of 362 sighting reports in 1967 alone. This was the total reported by people all over the British Isles who telephoned the Ministry or wrote letters about what they had seen.

In earlier years the totals investigated ranged from ninety-five (in 1966) down to a mere twenty-two in 1959. The grand total from 1959 to 1967 inclusive came to 808.

There is no department at the Ministry with special responsibility for investigating flying saucers. Other countries, notably America, may get hot under the collar about them, or appear to, but Whitehall remains unharrassed, even indifferent to the phenomena – at least on the surface. But in fact a great deal of care is taken to check up on reported sightings and satisfy the public. Most of the work is done by a secretarial department designated S4f (Air) which also deals with complaints about low flying, aircraft noise, etc.

What happens if you see some mysterious object in the sky and decide to telephone the Ministry about it? Whoever takes your call reaches for a form headed *Report of an Unidentified Flying Object* and starts to ask you questions from it which may help to classify the sighting and simplify later inquiries.

At the end of the conversation he will hope to have most of the following information:—

1 Date, time and duration of sighting.
2 A description including shape, size, colour and brightness of the object and whether it made any noise.
3 Your position at the time, geographically.

4 Whether you saw the object with the naked eye, binoculars or any other optical aid, and whether you succeeded in photographing it.
5 The direction in which the UFO was first seen, with any landmark which may help to pin-point the position.
6 Angle of sight (since estimated heights are unreliable).
7 Distance away (with landmarks for reference).
8 What movements the object made with speed estimates.
9 Weather conditions at the time, including details of cloud cover, mist, haze, etc.
10 Nearby objects on the ground such as telephone poles, lakes, dams, rivers, steeples, TV masts, and whether you were near an airfield, factory or building that might be floodlit.
11 Whether you have notified the police or any other local authority.
12 Your name and address, and whether you require a written statement of what the Ministry may be able to discover about the sighting.

With this information to hand, the secretarial staff are able to make immediate inquiries to the nearest radar establishment, Air Traffic Control, gliding clubs, the Royal Observatory, the police, Meteorological Office and anyone else who may be able to help identify the object. It was in this way, indeed, that they were able to satisfy themselves that the giant cone-shaped object seen hovering over Brixham in May 1967 was, in fact, a balloon. Some sightings are quickly cleared up, others may take days or even weeks, especially if they are not promptly reported, and some do not get cleared up at all – not that this causes the Ministry any embarrassment.

An analysis of the 808 sightings investigated to the end of 1967 shows that they fell into seven separate categories, as follows:—

1	Satellites and Debris	211
2	Balloons	92
3	Celestial objects (Venus etc.)	60

4	Meteorological and Natural Phenomena including mock suns and moons	72
5	Aircraft	226
6	Miscellaneous, reflections on clouds, hoaxes, etc.	63
7	Unexplained	84
	TOTAL	808

The analysis shows that over ten per cent of the sightings reported during the period covered were not explained, a not inconsiderable proportion indeed. But the Ministry's answer is not that these sightings were so remarkable as to defy any explanation. It is simply that there was insufficient information to go on. Either observers reported them too long after the event, or they were so vague about what they claimed to have seen that the Ministry investigators did not have a proper starting point for inquiries.

It is not, they say, that we utterly rule out the possibility that some UFOs may have an extra-terrestrial origin but we simply have no evidence that this is so. In reply to this, ufologists charge that the Ministry does not make enough effort to investigate the really mysterious UFOs and certainly does not use enough imagination in doing so. How can they if, as is admitted, UFO research is little more than a part-time job for someone?

There is more than enough evidence, they insist, to justify inquiries on the highest scientific level instead of employing a few 'casual' investigators to find comfortably mundane explanations for as many sightings as possible.

UFOs have been sighted in more than fifty countries but nowhere in the world is the saucer scene more spectacular than in America – the land which gave birth to the notion that the earth is being visited by craft and creatures from outer space. In the United States, as in Britain, UFOs have been reported by scientists, engineers, amateur astronomers, civil defence workers, teachers, clergymen, civilian and military pilots, professional and businessmen and ordinary citizens. There is no question that they have all seen *something*, whatever it may be. However, after two decades, during which more than 11,000 sightings have come under review, the official line of the

US Air Force is very much the same as that taken by Britain's Ministry of Defence. The official wording states that:

'No evidence has been received nor discovered which proves the existence and intraspace mobility of extra-terrestrial life.'

The Americans are not expecting the number of UFO sightings to diminish during the coming years. Rather the reverse. Those who take the view that there is nothing in the saucer phenomena worthy of serious consideration, blame newspapers and radios for fanning the flames of public imagination in the first place, and films, books and television plays about visitors from space for keeping it going.

Even the name Unidentified Flying Object is incriminated as implying that something seen in the sky was flying and was composed of solid material whereas it might have had no more substance than a mirage.

A brief glance at the history of the UFO in America shows that the first official body to undertake inquiries into the mystery was a department of the Air Force formed in 1947 (shortly after Kenneth Arnold reported his Mount Rainier sighting) to determine whether saucers posed any latent threat to national security. Then, in February 1948, 'Project Sign' was created to 'collect, evaluate and distribute information concerning UFO sightings'.

Eleven months later, after an analysis of 243 of the most well-documented reports, Project Sign indicated that 'no definite evidence was available to confirm or disprove the actual existence of unidentified flying objects as new or unknown types of aircraft'.

Towards the end of 1948, the project name was changed to 'Grudge' and 244 new reports came under review with the finding that: 'The phenomena present no threat to the security of the United States and the vast majority of sightings are misrepresentations of conventional objects'.

This was fine. But the saucers did not go away. In fact they loomed large enough as a defence problem in the 1950s for the Central Intelligence Agency (CIA) to take a long hard look at the phenomena, ostensibly to see if any UFOs were originating from sources overseas. Apparently this was not so, and such information as did not betray details of CIA organization and method was later made available to scientists, scholars and others interested in the study of UFOs.

The Air Force research organization was by then operating under the new name of Project Blue Book, which remains its official title. Its objectives were also enlarged. As well as trying to find out whether UFOs posed a threat to the security of the United States, the Project was charged with endeavouring to determine whether they exhibited any unique scientific information or advanced technology which could contribute to scientific or technical research.

The programme is carried out by the Aerial Phenomena Branch (Air Force Systems Command) at Wright-Patterson Air Force Base, Ohio. The Air Force insists that there is no censorship barrier preventing people from knowing what sightings are investigated and what conclusions are reached about them. It is stated, however, that there is an obligation to protect the names of people who volunteer information about sightings if that is their wish. In addition it is often felt necessary to withhold information that would give away the location of a classified installation or reveal secrets concerning the capabilities of certain aircraft and defence equipment.

No doubt all this is true, but it has given rise to allegations, from organizations which collect and publish information about flying saucers, that the Air Force is misleading the public about what is really going on and especially withholding information that would support claims that many UFOs come from extra-terrestrial sources.

A special article published in *The Airman*, the official magazine of the US Air Force, in the summer of 1967 to tell readers what was *really* known about UFOs, said they had been reported in all shapes and sizes. 'They resemble cigars, propellers, hats, pie pans, saucers and balls. Sizes vary from tiny objects estimated in inches to massive space ships reported to be 250 feet or more in diameter. The predominant colours are red, green, blue and white; however, the entire colour spectrum has been reported at one time or another. UFO sounds range from eerie silence to high-pitched, penetrating tones. Propulsion may be evidenced by flaming exhausts, or there may be no exhausts whatsoever. UFOs hover, zig-zag, move in any direction at variable speeds (one observer reported a UFO moving at 25,000 mph). Structures of reported UFOs fluctuate from solid to "invisible".

'Although UFOs are observed throughout the year,' the

article stated significantly, 'the largest number of sightings occur at night during the spring and summer when people spend more time out of doors.'

As for the positive identification of the vast majority of UFOs, it appeared that they had been explained away as unconventional aircraft, aircraft under uncommon weather conditions, aircraft with unusual external light patterns; meteorological and other high-altitude balloons; artificial earth satellites; flocks of birds; reflections of searchlights or headlights off clouds; reflection of sunlight from shiny surfaces; luminescent organisms, including in one case a firefly lodged between two adjacent panes of glass in an aircraft window; optical mirages and looming, lenticular cloud formations; ball lightning, sundogs, meteors; planets, especially Venus, bright stars and the aurora borealis.

'The planet Venus,' it was said, 'is frequently reported as a UFO when it is low down on the horizon. When viewed through the polluted air near the earth's surface, the planet appears to perform erratic manoeuvres and change colour.'

But the chief contributor to UFO sighting reports was the balloon. 'Several thousands are released each day from military and civilian airports, weather stations and research activities . . . These balloons sometimes appear to be flattened on top. At other times they appear to be saucer-shaped and to have lights mounted inside the bag itself due to the sun's rays reflecting through the material of the balloon.'

As for aircraft: 'When observed at high altitudes, aircraft can have appearances ranging from disc to rocket shapes due to the reflection of the sun on their bright surfaces. Vapour or condensation trails from jet aircraft will sometimes appear to glow fiery red or orange when reflecting sunlight. Afterburners from jet aircraft are often reported as UFOs since they can be seen from great distances when the aircraft cannot be seen.'

Project Blue Book officials say that the increase in the number of UFO sightings reported in recent years corresponds very significantly with the increase in artificial satellites put into orbit. During 1965, for example, 152 sightings were positively identified as Echo I, Echo II, Pegasus I, Pegasus II or Pegasus III. Even the UFOs which astronauts sighted during their Gemini flights were later proved to be satellites or parts of satellites launched from earth. Besides this, they say, although vast expanses of the sky over the United States have been under surveillance on clear nights in recent years, astronomers have not detected a single movement suggesting that a vehicle of unknown origin was approaching the earth. And the 'mysterious' blips that sometimes appear on radar screens and then vanish again are said to be no more than echoes from rain clouds and temperature inversions – when an upper layer of air is warmer than the layer immediately beneath it.

After more than twenty years of investigation, Project Blue Book officials say the US Air Force does not have a single photograph or film strip of a UFO. Every photograph of an alleged UFO submitted for analysis has turned out to be an astronomical body, balloon, lens flare, emulsion flaw, double negative or photographic defect, while a small percentage have been hoaxes.

All the same, it does not appear that the Americans are satisfied that they have got the full measure of the UFO for, after looking into the problem in 1966, the Air Force Scientific Advisory Board recommended that research should be expanded to include investigation of selected sightings by independent scientists.

As a result, the Secretary of the Air Force announced on 7 October 1966, that Colorado University had been chosen to conduct independent inquiries into flying saucer reports. The sum of $300,000 was to be spent on a research programme lasting fifteen months.

The University team, headed by Dr Edward Condon, professor of physics and former head of the US National Bureau of Standards, were to have access to Project Blue Book files and freedom to follow whatever lines of study they fancied. They were also to make their findings public at the end of the inquiry.

At the same time as this announcement was made, it was revealed that an impressive nucleus of top American scientists was pressing for an even greater attack on the UFO problem. What they wanted was not a limited, academic type of inquiry such as they expected to be made by the Condon team, but a country-wide effort involving the resources of the National Aeronautics and Space Administration. A leading figure in this group of scientists was Dr J. Allen Hynek, an astrophysicist from North Western University near Chicago and the Air Force's chief consultant on UFO matters.

For twenty years Dr Hynek, as a working member of the Project Blue Book, had been regarded as an opponent of flying saucers, inclined to dismiss the UFO phenomena as a product of public imagination and misinterpretation. But now, it appeared, he was so impressed by the enormous collection of evidence from reliable witnesses that he had abruptly changed sides. Out in support of him had come the no less distinguished figure of Dr James McDonald, a professor in the University of Arizona's department of meteorology and senior physicist at the university's Institute of Atmospheric Physics.

'Unidentified flying objects,' said Dr McDonald, 'represent the greatest scientific problem of our time.' The possibility that they come from outside the earth must be given extremely serious scientific attention.

Accusing the United States Air Force of gross neglect and incompetence in dealing with the problem, Dr McDonald said that reports of UFO sightings published in newspapers represented only the 'tip of an iceberg'. Project Blue Book, he alleged, had had the effect of setting back serious scientific study of UFOs by many years. The Air Force had become convinced by its own propaganda. Scientists had been led to believe that UFO reports were being effectively checked and shown to be due to natural phenomena. It was not that there was a conspiracy to hush up the truth. The big cover-up was just a big foul-up.

Dr McDonald traced the trouble back to 1953 when a small panel of scientists, after studying a sample of UFO reports, decided that there was no evidence that they were 'artefacts of a hostile foreign power'. After that conclusion, he alleged, UFOs were considered to be of no more interest, and a systematic programme of debunking flying saucers was started with a view to reducing the number of what the CIA regarded as irrelevant reports about airborne objects.

The Project Blue Book office, Dr McDonald declared, consisted of three men, a major, a sergeant and a secretary. It was run as 'an extremely low priority project', yet it frequently issued authoritative sounding 'scientific explanations' of UFO sightings which were often scientifically outrageous. As for the Colorado University inquiry, he could see no more in it than an attempt by the Air Force to get rid of what it believed to be a public relations problem rather than a scientific one.

Flying saucers have often been denounced and more often ridiculed, but somehow they have always managed to bounce back. After twenty years indeed they have become a 'respectable' topic of conversation among educated people, and I predict that it will be many years before any satisfactory solution to the mystery is obtained.

Indeed, we may have to wait until somebody from an alien planet actually lands here and freely declares himself to be a visitor from outer space . . . if this has not been done already.

15

The Colorado University Report

The Colorado University Report on UFOs was published in January 1969. It was in three volumes and numbered nearly 1,500 pages. It was bleak and uncompromising.

It stated flatly that there were no such things as flying saucers and never had been. Nearly all the UFO sightings, said the report, were related to ordinary objects such as aircraft, satellites, balloons, street lights, clouds or other natural phenomena. To pursue the matter further on anything but a limited scale would be a waste of money and time.

The scientific committee headed by Professor Edward Condon said they had found no evidence whatever for the claim that any UFOs are spacecraft visiting earth from another civilization. They dismissed as ludicrous the notion that American authorities had captured extra-terrestrial craft and were keeping quiet about it.

Not the least worrying aspect of the UFO business, said the Condon Committee, was its effect on schoolchildren. It recommended that teachers should encourage subjects to study astronomy, meteorology and other conventional subjects rather than read about UFOs. 'We feel,' said Professor Condon, 'that children are educationally harmed by absorbing unsound and erroneous material as if it were scientifically well-founded'.

Admitting that between 1961 and 1966 American astronauts had reported seeing UFOs, the Committee said that 'nothing was seen that could be construed as a "flying saucer" or manned vehicle from outer space.' They were satisfied that UFOs did not constitute any hazard or threat to national security and felt there was no need for the United States Government to establish a new agency to study the phenomena. On the other hand there was no reason why the Defence Department, particularly the Air Force, should not continue routine evaluation of UFO sightings. Since it appeared that there were gaps in existing knowledge about atmospheric optics, radio wave movements and electricity, further studies might lead to improving the safety of aircraft flights. UFO reports and beliefs might also be of interest to social scientists and communications specialists.

On the face of it the Condon Committee's report just about wrapped up the whole mystery. But hardly had the first inklings of what it contained become known then there were sounds of dissension. Not everybody, it seemed, was going to accept the findings as final. Under the headline: 'UFO STUDY STARTS NEW CONTROVERSY' *The Times* commented: 'In spite of two years and $500,000 (£208,000) spent by the United States Air Force on a study of Unidentified Flying Objects by the University of Colorado, the controversy will not die down'.

The Times backed up this prediction by revealing that from the outset serious differences of opinion existed between American scientists concerning the way the Colorado study should be carried out and that as a result some of the original team had been dismissed, including Dr David Saunders, joint principal investigator. Dr Saunders was quoted as saying about the Condon report: 'It is inconceivable that it can be anything but a stone stew. No matter how long it is, what it includes, how it is said or what it recommends, it will lack the essential element of credibility'.

Dr Saunders, *The Times* said, had written a paperback book (presumably criticizing the work of the Condon Committee) to coincide with the release of the report. Dr Saunders was claiming, it appeared, that his and other departures from the project were the result of a dispute over a memorandum by Mr Robert Low, the original co-ordinator of the project. However, Dr Saunders did not think the project had been a total failure. The study of UFOs was now considered to be more respectable than it had been two years earlier. Some necessary concepts and models had been developed and there were a few fresh facts.

There was no doubt, however, that a major row was building up in America. Another newspaper quoted Major Donald Keyhoe, director of the 12,000-member National Investigations Committee on Aerial Phenomena as saying: 'We are publicly challenging the attempt to dismiss UFOs. Dr Condon started off as a non-believer and made his findings fit his beliefs.'